FASHION
V
SPORT

FASHION V SPORT

Sponsored by

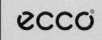

ECCO, the global footwear brand with a reputation for combining style and comfort, is proud to sponsor the V&A's contemporary exhibition Fashion V Sport.

As an innovator within the world of active, casual and formal footwear, ECCO takes great interest in how design and technical innovation in both fashion and sportswear can interact to create a unique style that crosses both genres.

We hope that visitors to the display and readers of this accompanying book will be intrigued by the insights reflected within this exciting exhibition that examines this complex relationship.

David Sleigh, Managing Director

First published by V&A Publishing, 2008
V&A Publishing, Victoria and Albert Museum, South Kensington, London, SW7 2RL

Distributed in North America by
Harry N. Abrams, Inc., New York

© The Board of Trustees of the Victoria and Albert Museum

The moral right of the authors has been asserted.

Paperback edition
ISBN-13 978 1 85177 533 0
Library of Congress Number 2007935515

10 9 8 7 6 5 4 3 2 1
2012 2011 2010 2009 2008

A catalogue record for this book is available from the British Library.

Every effort has been made to seek permission to reproduce those images whose copyright does not reside with the V&A, and we are grateful to the individuals and institutions who have assisted in this task. Any omissions are entirely unintentional, and the details should be addressed to V&A Publications.

Front cover illustration: Based on a photograph by Adam Hammond.

Back cover illustrations, left to right: Dries van Noten, Spring/Summer 2007 (p.89); Matt Walsh at the launch of the Speedo Fastskin FSII, 2004 (p.41); Niyi in Adicolour black series, Keith Haring and Jeremy Scott suit pants, 2006 (p.53); Thierry Henry in Tommy Hilfiger, 2007 (p.10).

Printed in Singapore.

V&A Publishing
Victoria and Albert Museum
South Kensington
London SW7 2RL
www.vam.ac.uk

ACKNOWLEDGEMENTS

First and foremost, I am deeply grateful to the designers, photographers and contributors who generously gave their time, information, ideas and images to this publication. Additionally, for their boundless assistance, I would like to thank the many individuals who have acted as points of liaison between myself and the contributors: Lucy Beeden at Kim Jones, Matthew Boulé at Visvim, Jackie Dunning at Microzine, Yasuhiro Kaji at Miharayasuhiro, Lucie Kershaw at Exposure, Louise Lewer and Nic Galway at Adidas and Yurika Morita at SOPHNET. I would also like to express gratitude to Ben Lau, Jodi Muter and David Olaniyi for their enthusiastic involvement in discreet aspects of this publication.

I would like to express my sincere gratitude to ECCO Shoes, the sponsors of Fashion V Sport, for their backing of and enthusiasm for the project. Similarly, I want to thank David Lowbridge for the wonderful design of this book and his never-ending patience throughout the design and editing process. For their continued support, I am indebted to numerous current and former colleagues at the Victoria & Albert Museum, especially Frances Ambler, Christopher Breward, Ulrich Lehmann, Louise Shannon and Oliver Winchester. At this point, I would especially like to thank Shaun Cole and Mary Butler for giving me the opportunity to tackle this fascinating subject.

In particular, I am thankful to Takeharu Sato, Yasuyuki Takaki, Angela Reynolds and Koichiro Yamamoto for facilitating and enabling my research in Tokyo. I would like to express my genuine gratitude to Tony Charalambous, without whose assistance in researching and sourcing images, this book would have not been possible. Finally, I am obliged to numerous people who have listened to and directed me throughout the process of editing and writing this book; particularly Michelle Jones, who has spent many hours talking to me during the early concept development and has read and commented on many drafts of this book, and most of all Brett Booth, who has endured even more hours of debating the visual and textual content of this book and the exhibition it accompanies.

INTRODUCTION

THE GLOBAL AND THE LOCAL

LIGAYA SALAZAR

As sportswear has become a universal part of the modern wardrobe, with trainers and tracksuits often more readily worn than suits and skirts, *Fashion V Sport* sets out to explore the origins and motivations underlying this seemingly ubiquitous way of dressing by examining the relationship between fashion and sportswear. Frequently seen as diametrically opposed ends of cultural production, these two industries have recently collaborated increasingly closely in the design and marketing of apparel and shoes. Most of these collaborations were formed during the last 10 years: Yasuhiro Mihara and Puma officially launched in 2000, Yohji Yamamoto and Adidas's Y-3 in 2002 and Kim Jones and Umbro in 2004, to name just a few; but rather than signalling the beginning of a relationship between these two industries, they signal the culmination of a long-standing interaction.

It is the intention of this exhibition and book to unravel some of the intertwining influences that the fashion and sport industries have had on each other by exploring the reciprocal nature of their relationship in recent years. Sportswear as defined here encompasses the entire spectrum, ranging from functional sportswear to sports-inspired designer clothes. *Fashion V Sport* attempts to unpick the complex, often confusing and tense correlation between how the industries are perceived through marketing and advertising and how their products are consumed and worn.

While the direct engagement of sports brands with fashion designers or fashionable design practice is a relatively

new phenomenon, the influence of sporting tradition and innovation on the development of fashion has many historical precedents that have made sport, as fashion historian Elizabeth Wilson proclaims, 'possibly the most important twentieth-century influence on fashion'.[1] This book opens with Christopher Breward's analysis of the perceived dichotomy between the inherent timelessness of sport and the ever-changing nature of fashion in his chapter 'Pure Gesture'. With reference to literary critic Roland Barthes' notion of the 'pure gesture', taken from his essay on 'The World of Wrestling' in which he likens wrestlers to god-like beings, Breward explores the history of the relationship between the two design spheres, and their common ground – including their reliance on tradition and innovation, their pursuit of playfulness, shared interest in the human form and production of spectacle.

Thierry Henry promoting his Tommy Hilfiger capsule
collection in aid of The One 4 All Foundation, 2007.
Photograph by David Bailey

Although sportswear is a global phenomenon, it is often seen as inherently American. Historically, as more hierarchical and formal traditions of dressing remained engrained in Europe, designers in the US were able to introduce a more democratic approach to dressing. As curator Richard Martin states in the catalogue to his 1998 exhibition at the Metropolitan Museum of Art in New York, aptly titled 'American Ingenuity':

Fashion in America was logical and answerable to the will of the women who wore it. Implicitly or explicitly, American fashion addressed a democracy, whereas traditional Paris-based fashion was authoritarian and imposed on women, willing or not.[2]

It is this tendency to welcome a more 'democratic' fashion that, in terms of clothes design, facilitated the life of the consumer, since the clothes became more and more practical and informal. The rationality in their design and the simplicity of their construction also suited mass-production techniques. Eventually clothes design became simple to the extent that it was necessary to develop modern marketing and branding as garments had become supposedly indistinguishable. As fashion historian Jennifer Craik concludes, 'Sportswear is, then, an intrinsically American phenomenon, albeit one that has travelled globally, including back to Europe.'[3]

It is the globalization of this supposedly American style of dressing that plays a particularly pertinent role in the perceived proximity of the fashion and sportswear industries. When one considers American sports brands such as Nike – described by anthropologist Ian Skoggard as a 'marketing firm which owns no factories to speak of and instead concentrates solely on design and marketing'[4] – which until recently dominated the athletic shoe market worldwide, it is natural to assume that the relationship between fashion and sport is global. Especially since its most visible, and probably most obvious, manifestations are the global fashion advertising campaigns headed by famous sports players such as David James for Armani, David Beckham for Police, Cristiano Ronaldo for Pepe and Thierry Henry for Tommy Hilfiger.

However, recent developments within the retailing practice of sportswear, and sport/fashion collaborations in particular, seem to suggest otherwise. When Nike opened its first flagship store close to its headquarters in Portland, Oregon back in 1990, the imposing architecture and the mere fact it was called 'Niketown' declared the brand's intention and purpose: a superbrand dedicated to performance sports apparel and shoes, its retail outlet a 'town', leaving no need for the consumer to go anywhere else to buy the best sports-related goods. Skoggard described the New York flagship store as a 'shrine for athletes and athleticism', including a terracotta inlaid floor depicting 'a map of the world with a Nike Town "swoosh" anagram superimposed over it', a clear indication of what it intended the future to hold for Nike. Yet, in the intervening years, something changed. This was not merely as a consequence of Naomi Klein's influential book *No Logo*, published in 2000, which laid bare the unethical production practices of superbrands such as Nike and other

global corporations; nor was it just that, as journalist Geraldine Bedell found, customers were 'involved in much more of a dialogue with brands than was realised a few years ago'.[5] Instead it was a combination of factors that evidently led to a shift in how sports brands were perceived, which meant that they had to react and adapt their retail and marketing practices.

Puma was one of the first to acknowledge that, as Antonio Bertone, their global director of brand management, stated, 'people become desensitised if the only message you give them is that your trainers are the latest and greatest'. He continued: 'The current generation has grown up with trainers: they already know they're supposed to make you run faster and jump higher.'[6] Now frequently listed as one of the major sports brands, Puma was also the first to embrace the status and practices of a fashion brand fully. In 2005 it opened the multi-branded Puma Black Store in New York, which only retails collaborative and exclusive dedicated sport fashion products. These include its '96 Hours' range designed by Neil Barrett, and its custom-made trainers by Italian leather goods company Schedoni. In 2007 it opened another Black Store in Tokyo, and in the same year the company was bought by multi-brand luxury goods conglomerate PPR, which also owns Yves Saint Laurent, Balenciaga and Gucci, thus indicating its further shift away from sports goods manufacturer towards fashion company.

The role the knowledgeable and fashionable consumer plays in all this is considerable. What Skoggard describes as 'flexible consumption'[7] regarding Nike's annual increase in designs ('from 1971... to 1989, the average life of its shoe design decreased from seven years to ten months')[8] seems to have taken on a new meaning within the retail practices of the fashionable sportswear industry in recent years. Now, it is not enough to produce ever more designs each year, they also have to be conveyed to the consumer differently. An interesting manifestation of this is the entirely unbranded Adidas shop, opened in 2004 near London's Carnaby Street, merely called '6 Newburgh Street', its stated intention to 'function as a revolutionary brand platform that will position, communicate and prove that Adidas is the authentic, original sportswear brand'.[9] Another is Umbro's fashionable guerrilla shop which opened the same year in the East End of London and the 'exhibition' displaying the Umbro by Kim Jones collection alongside a series of photographs for the launch of the second issue of fashion magazine *Fantastic Man* in Stockholm in 2005. Identified by one of the many trendspotting agencies as part of a larger trend dubbed 'pop-up retail', this new trend has been adopted by companies as varied as Comme des Garçons, with its travelling guerrilla store launched in Berlin in 2004, and Nike, with its 2007 temporary store celebrating its Air Force shoe's 25th birthday in Tokyo's fashionable Harajuku district.

What is interesting about this shift is that it appears to subvert globalization by diversifying the consumer experience of the brand locally or by differentiating the brand into small segments, as is exemplified by Puma's 13 non-sport-specific sub-brands,

6

and by both the Nike ID initiative and Reebok's Rbk custom (where consumers are invited to create their own individual trainer). Localized marketing initiatives such as the guerrilla stores intend to increase brand credibility and forge links between the consumer and the brand, but as these events happen globally, this is actually only a perceived 'localization'.

All this could be seen as the industry's desperate or, perhaps, very intelligent, attempt to feed what Elizabeth Wilson describes as the contemporary consumer's 'mad attention to details that are in themselves meaningless, to destroy the surrounding ennui, to create meaning out of emptiness and impose the imperative self on the alien, computerized routines of dominant culture'.[10] Describing countercultural fashions in the 1980s, her statement finds an absurdly twisted new meaning in the 2000s as the 'mad attention to details' once invented and employed by groups of young people to rebel against the establishment are now instantly catered for by the establishment itself, in a fashionable guise.

Hence, the 'local' urban environment of the fashionable city performs two important functions in this development, as a provider of consumables and as a stage for consumers to perform their stylistic adaptation of clothes. The notion that the shopping streets of a city are also a performance space is not new to the twenty-first century: from the nineteenth century onwards the streets have provided an environment where 'new and more complicated "codes of dress" developed'.[11] Even though the death of the city sphere was mourned by many commentators in the 1990s as a consequence of the increasing popularity of TV retail and shopping malls (and again now, through the possibilities of the internet), it seems that the metropolis is still is crucial to the formation of new styles.[12] Consuming in the contemporary urban space has become even more differentiated, it seems, precisely because the dominant experience of the high street has become so homogenized. And the 'virtual space' has actually both supported and subverted these differentiation processes with specialized websites and blogs reviewing the latest product and indicating where to find it. These websites and blogs in particular, but also the internet in general, have thus facilitated the aforementioned system of 'flexible consumption'.

The speed with which many fashion and sports apparel brands are able either to simulate or adapt what people wear in the many global cities is due to the increasing popularity of what journalist Malcolm Gladwell labelled 'coolhunters'.[13] These are either separate companies or integrated departments – though usually highly dependent on individuals who are in the 'fashionable know' – such as Nike's Consumer Insight Teams, whose sole purpose is to spot the next cool thing and find ways to feed it into the next design or colourway. The clothes and styles performed by people on the streets of global cities – and this is particularly true for sports-inspired apparel and shoes – are therefore especially important as inspiration for both sportswear brands and fashion designers alike. Two of the most explicit recent examples of this are Adidas's lace

jewellery, a take on popular ways of accessorizing the laces of trainers, and Converse's All Stars, fitted with two-coloured tongues so that they can be worn showing the differently coloured inside.

This is precisely where the paradox of the present situation lies: the local consumer is both unknowing collaborator and victim of a sportswear industry that has not only adopted a fashionable guise, but also fully integrated the fashion cycle into its practice. Thus, *Fashion V Sport* sets out to examine contemporary developments through the inherent contradictions within the relationship between fashion and sport. The tensions of this relationship are reflected in the four sections, DARE: Tradition V Innovation, DISPLAY: Uniformity V Individuality, PLAY: Performance V Performativity, and DESIRE: Narcissism and Obsession. Each of the first three highlights a supposed opposition and explores the creative energy such tensions produce. In the fourth section, however, the pairing of the two words 'Narcissism' and 'Obsession' is complementary, part of the section examines one of the most striking collaborative ventures of the two industries: pairing the athletic body of the sporting hero and the marketing of menswear. The other part looks at the obsession it triggers both with sport itself and the consumables linked to it. Consequently this structure reveals the intention of the exhibition: to extract some of the reasons for the proximity of these two industries now, not through a smooth historical narrative – which could not do justice to the complexity of the subject matter at hand – but through a probing thematic investigation.

PURE
GESTURE

REFLECTIONS ON THE HISTORIES OF SPORT AND FASHION

CHRISTOPHER BREWARD

When the hero or the villain of the drama… leaves the wrestling hall, impassive, anonymous, carrying a small suitcase and arm in arm with his wife, no one can doubt that wrestling holds that power of transmutation which is common to the Spectacle and to Religious Worship. In the ring, and even in the depths of their voluntary ignominy, wrestlers remain gods because they are, for a few moments, the key which opens Nature, the pure gesture which separates Good from Evil, and unveils the form of a Justice which is at last intelligible.[1]

When Roland Barthes' observations on 'The World of Wrestling' were published in his *Mythologies* collection of essays in 1952, he made reference to its transcendental, quasi-religious status. Like many competitive sports, but perhaps more intensely than most, modern wrestling appeared to connect the spectator directly back to the elemental function of the ancient games, partaking in Barthes' words 'of the nature of the great solar spectacles, Greek drama and bullfights: in both, a light without shadow generates an emotion without reserve'.[2] These are not uncommon reflections, and it comes as no surprise that the figure of the victorious sports man or woman has so consistently been positioned as an icon of Platonic perfection in Western art and literature. It is no coincidence that such figures are generally depicted naked or near-naked, without the encumbrance of clothing. Indeed Barthes usefully highlights the image of the retiring wrestler, his costume hidden in a suitcase – an anonymized, ignominious everyman, made mortal again by a civilian suit. Fashion, with its adherence to ephemeral cycles of taste

and the rhythms of the marketplace, would thus seem to stand in opposition to the timeless qualities of athleticism. Moreover, in other essays in the same collection, Barthes deliberately emphasizes the superficial attractions of fashionable commodity forms, attractions that are far removed from the natural 'grandiloquence' of the sporting hero. The 'pure gesture' of athletic prowess simply magnifies the impure character of a contemporary culture in thrall to base fashion.

And yet, as this piece will suggest, the links between the worlds of fashion and sport are much stronger than such symbolic contrasts might indicate. In fact, several social histories of modern sport make reference to a shared commercial context, arguing that a reification of the body binds the two fields together, positioning them as twin motors of consumer culture. Sports sociologist John Hargreaves goes so far as to claim that 'the body is clearly an object of crucial importance in consumer culture and its supply industries; and sports, together with fashion, eating and drinking outside the home, cooking, dieting, keep fit therapy… advertising imagery, and a battery of aids to sexual attractiveness, are deployed in a constantly elaborating programme whose objective is the production of the new, "normalized" individual'.[3] He also sets up a number of identifying characteristics of sport that could just as well be utilized in a definition of modern fashion. These include an emphasis on play and pleasure, a reliance on 'elaborate codes and statutes', the production of a sense of anticipation and excitement, a dramatic quality providing opportunity 'for discourse on some of the basic themes of social life',

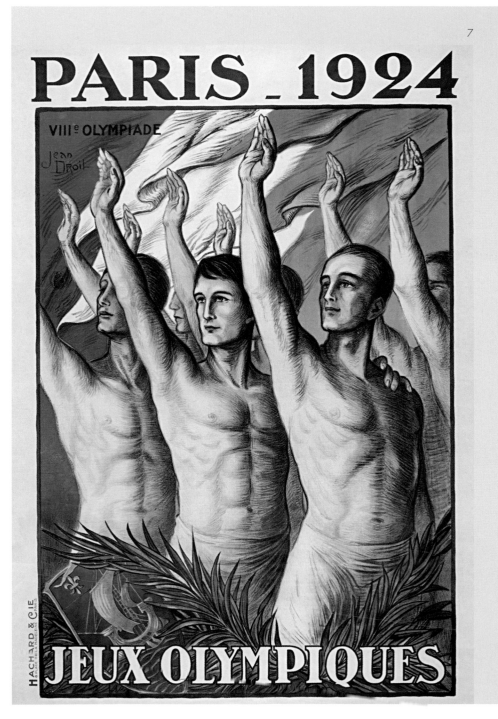

7

a related ritualistic content, and, as noted, a positioning of the body as 'the most striking symbol as well as the material core of sporting activity'.[4]

The clothing-focused themes of this book are not so distant from Hargreaves' characteristics – the challenge of innovation where materials and techniques are honed for competitive advantage, the dramatic struggle between uniformity and individuality, the spectacle of sporting and sartorial performance and the ritualistic fetishization of physical perfection all cohere to produce a sense of the modern subject informed by the common concerns of fashion and sport. But besides recognizing these broad conceptual connections, it is also important to acknowledge the historical transformations that have allowed such alliances to flourish. The task of the following sections is to identify precedents, to show how the contemporary prominence of fashion/sport owes its hegemony to earlier models.

First, a brief consideration of the continuities and ruptures in the history of modern leisure pursuits that underpinned the key technical, aesthetic and philosophical developments in the evolution of clothing for sport and sporting fashions. In nineteenth and early twentieth-century Europe and America, but particularly in late Victorian Britain, urban societies witnessed a 'scramble for sport'.[5] Historian John Lowerson describes how this scramble was informed by broader trends. Physical recreation, like related facets of material culture, became a means by which an increasingly stratified social structure (marked along the lines of class, gender, ethnicity and age) was codified and understood. Furthermore, the growing popularity of sports made them an attractive focus for entrepreneurship as Britain gradually shifted from a manufacturing towards a service economy. Naturally this encouraged an increasing commercialization of sport that also reflected the changing attitudes of growing numbers of consumers towards their use of free time, the ways in which they inhabited private and public space and the opportunities for spending their wages. Finally, in tandem with the rise in sports-related venture capitalism, sporting activity embodied the core moral values of Victorian constructs of 'respectability'. These included the concepts of 'self-help' and 'self-control', and were summed up in the popular motto *mens sana in corpore sano* ('a healthy mind in a healthy body'). It is significant that such values, rooted as they were in the principles of gentlemanly amateurism, stood in opposition to increasing commercialization.[6]

In addition to these socially located changes, the emergence of a modern sports economy was stimulated by specific institutional and professional interests – most importantly, the rise of a national and international media and advertising industry, where individual competitors could be promoted as celebrities and teams positioned as assets. This more American model, 'influenced by the principles of the commercial entertainment industry', has since tended to dominate in the twentieth and twenty-first centuries. It is a change that has been described by sports sociologist John Horne as 'a shift from amateur Olympism to Prolympism', echoing a gradual decline of philanthropic and state support for sporting initiatives and an increasing reliance 'on modern capitalist management and marketing techniques'.[7]

A very similar pattern could be claimed for the development of the modern fashion industry over the same period. Clothing operated as primary indicator of social status, occupation and moral rectitude in nineteenth-century society. Its meanings were also influenced by the potential of mass-reproduction – so that by the mid-twentieth century fashion could be considered as much an aspect of popular culture as football or tennis. In this sense one might compare the shift from amateurism to professionalization, and from local to global concerns in the organization of sport, with the gradual decline of bespoke methods of clothing manufacture and the rise of fashion's symbolic reach as brand rather than individualized material product.[8] Most importantly, however, the two sectors came together at this time in their shared concerns with the concepts of modernity, glamour and the celebration of the heroic, rationalized body. As British *Vogue* commented in 1926, 'Sport has more to do than anything else with the evolution of the modern mode; … there is only one thing of which everyone is convinced… and that is the perfection of the adaptation to the needs of the game which modern dress has evolved.'[9]

8   Norfolk jacket. Checked tweed, with sateen
    and striped cotton lining and buttons of horn.
    Hand- and machine-sewn. British, c.1890–1900.
    V&A: T.356-1984
9   Vexed Generation, 'Vexed Parka', ballistics
    nylon with neoprene. Autumn/Winter 1995–6.
    Loan from Vexed Generation

DARE

8

The accomplishment of that perfect fit
between functionality, modernity and
fashionability to which *Vogue* referred,
which found its most compelling
manifestation in early twentieth-century
sportswear, evolved out of an earlier
negotiation between the competing
demands of respectability, display and
comfort that dictated the look of the late
nineteenth-century male wardrobe. Social
historian Brent Shannon, in his work on
men, dress and consumer culture in Victorian
and Edwardian Britain, suggests that 'this
newfound appreciation of sartorial comfort
reflected a larger… cultural shift in social
values that witnessed an exuberant
celebration of a rugged, vigorous, athletic
masculinity'. Such a shift, reflecting fears
about the decline of Empire and the
growing 'feminization' of English society,
ran in parallel with the commodification of
sports activities, resulting in 'the radical
transformation of men's fashions… as well
as of the entire cultural ideal of the male
body'. Shannon cites one 1901 etiquette
guide that sets the perfect 'man of today'
in sharp focus. He 'is slim, athletic but not
burly… His shoulders are broad (padding
has been done away with), his limbs are
sturdy, and he affects a quick, brisk walk.
Anglomaniacs lengthen the step to a
pronounced stride. All live much in the open
air, and clothes are worn easier, looser,
and more comfortable than heretofore…
It is a period of aesthetic athletes.'[10]

If any garment was suggestive of the
'aesthetic athlete', it was surely the Norfolk
jacket – an item that combined up-to-date
and fit-for-purpose functionality with the
romantic associations of rugged manly
pursuits and sublime moorland settings.

FASHION V SPORT

The traditional aristocratic associations of the item were founded in its supposed invention for the Duke of Norfolk in the 1860s as an adaptable, hard-wearing outfit for estate pursuits. By the 1880s it had entered into middle-class wardrobes where its protective tweed textile, reinforced structure and capacious pockets lent it to a variety of uses, including bicycling, fishing, shooting, golf and walking. An example in the V&A's collections boasts the sort of gadget-like features, including a versatile expanding belt and button-up lapels, that would not seem out of place on performance-led leisure/sports outfits produced a hundred years later.[11] The 'Vexed Parka' introduced by Vexed Generation for Autumn/Winter 1995–6, with its ballistics, fire- and knife-proof nylon/neoprene construction and pockets designed for holding a gas mask, is an unsettling update on underlying Norfolk jacket principles; here, however, the sport envisaged relates to the crime and riot-torn streets of a dystopian twenty-first century city rather than the idyllic game-reserves of the Scottish highlands.[12]

At the same time that such items as the Norfolk jacket were introducing the aesthetics of the sporting life into civilian dress, organized sport was witnessing the reverse trend: the gradual adaptation of traditional everyday dress for service as specialized uniforms suited to the rules and regulations of particular games. As fashion theorist Jennifer Craik has pointed out, this led to a form of stylistic fossilization in some 'genteel' sports such as cricket, where 'by the 1860s [the adoption of] white flannels, white shirt, team blazer, Arran-style knitted pullovers and… cap – was standardized

and remained the convention for over a century. This outfit was not always practical – white trousers were hard to clean… caps gave little shade from the sun… and long trousers were hot, particularly when cricket became an obsession in British colonies. Yet, changes were resisted.'[13] The vivid symbolism of a rather prissy purity – so neatly encapsulated in a letter of 1823 from a female spectator witnessing the preening of the Marylebone Cricket Club in action, 'dressed in tight white jackets (the Apollo Belvedere could not bear the hideous disguise of a cricket-jacket), with neck cloths primly tied round their throats… japanned shoes, silk stockings and gloves' – was seemingly more enduring than any concessions to function-led innovation.[14]

The more democratic sport of football followed another, though not dissimilar path, where items of everyday dress were initially worn for play. While a tougher aesthetic prevailed than in cricket, a tension between the 'manliness' of the sport and a tendency to personal display was still prevalent, as a *Handbook to Football*, published in 1867, made clear: 'Your hard workers at football gird up their loins with a broad leather belt, and donning their oldest and dirtiest trousers, and oldest and dirtiest tight jersey, with no covering on their heads and a faithful and trusty pair of boots on their feet… Be that as it may, there is the light division to be thought of, and the pretty Football players… Well, for such as these, useful and excellent fellows in their way, the prettiest costume is a coloured velvet cap with a tassel, a tight striped jersey, white flannel trousers, boots a discretion…'[15] Eventually the modern team strip, which emerged around the time of the First World

11 *Football Weekly*, 17 May 1968.
V&A: AAD/1985/3/2/582/1

War, combined elements of both trends, favouring all the forward-looking advantages provided by light fabrics and a dynamic cut adapted for mobility, whilst retaining the traditional heraldic colours and heroic aspects that lent the sport its accessible glamour. As a commentator in the late 1960s noted: 'basically the dress of the immediately pre-Great War footballer was what it still is today – new materials are in use, shorts have got shorter, boots have got lighter, but photographs of players of the 1900s and 1960s seem very much alike.'[16]

On one level, this sporting model of sartorial evolution may seem to have little in common with the rapid and apparently irrational emergence of new fashions in the wider consumer culture, yet the idea of the player's uniform as an alliance of unchanging traditions and progressive innovation is not so far removed from Walter Benjamin's influential interpretation of modern fashion's workings. Discussed by fashion theorist Ulrich Lehmann, here 'fashion fuses the thesis (the eternal or classical ideal) with its antithesis (the openly contemporary)'.[17] In the history of dressing for sport we appear to have the perfect illustration of this phenomenon, where the forces of classicism and novelty operate together through the concept of fashion as a cyclical process – simultaneously looking forwards and back: small wonder that the two fields have become progressively intertwined.

11

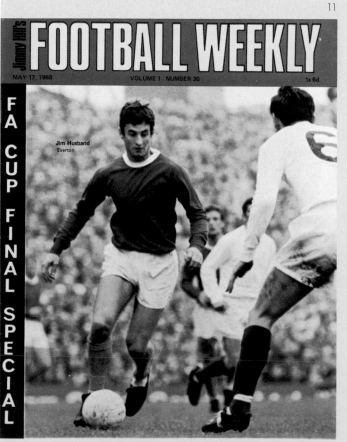

DISPLAY

Whilst the development of sporting dress in the nineteenth century was characterized by the competing influences of tradition and innovation, sartorial trends in the first half of the twentieth century witnessed a new emphasis on the rising sports star that sat alongside the celebration of a powerful cult of physical uniformity. Both phenomena looked towards the symbol of the heroic athlete's body as a source of inspiration and saw in the redesign of sports uniforms and fashionable clothing the potential for reforming contemporary life and embracing the energy of modernity.[18] Such powerful motors of change also proved to be instrumental in the emergence of the idea of the sportswear brand as the material encapsulation of a sport/fashion ideology that could be marketed and reproduced across national and cultural boundaries.

One of the underpinning principles of branding is the concept of universality – the suppression of the specific or the individual in favour of the collective.[19] In the matter of clothing, simplification of cut and standardization of manufacture are a necessary precondition for 'universalization', and in the 1920s and 1930s functional dress adapted for physical exertion became an obvious vehicle through which artists, philosophers, designers and even progressive clothing manufacturers could explore these themes. Avant-garde movements in Communist Russia and Fascist Italy and Germany were fascinated by the ways in which sports uniforms in particular lent themselves to the service of often disturbing ideologies. As art historian Radu Stern suggests: '…all totalitarian leaders have been fond of sport. The totalitarian state claimed not only the soul of its citizens but also their bodies. Considered an affair of state in the Soviet era, sport was a favourite subject for agitprop; physical exercise was almost a revolutionary duty. Quite often, stadiums were used not only as sports fields but also as a place for celebrating the mass of uniform thinking, whether in Moscow or Nuremburg.'[20]

In the field of clothing design, some of this thinking had a longer, more benign history. In the 1880s, for example, Dr Gustave Jaeger succeeded in marrying the theoretical imperatives of dress reform with his own practice as a successful garment manufacturer and retailer. He prioritized health over transient fashion in his influential writings, although it was understood that the pursuit of hygienic ideals in dress would automatically give rise to pleasing visual effects. Jaeger's original 'system' of dressing was based on the 'scientific' premise that the wearing of undyed woollen fibres next to the skin would aid the dispersion of bodily poisons and allow the skin to breathe freely. In terms of structure, clothing that did not constrain physical exercise and followed rational principles of construction and design was favoured, and although such principles undoubtedly shifted with the times, by the 1930s Jaeger fashions were still associated with the active and egalitarian circumstances of contemporary life rather than the effete dictates of Paris.[21] An advertisement for a trim Jaeger 'dungaree suit' of 1936, designed by pioneering woman motor-racer Kay Petrie, captures this sense of progressivism and echoes the promotion of *prozodezhda* (utilitarian overalls 'created for various spheres of labour, physical exercises, in the theatre, for biomechanics – where there is a precise

JAEGER AND KAY PETRIE

MAKE A RACING CHANGE

Jaeger are the all-round
champions for sports clothes.
Jaeger Tennis clothes are
designed by a Tennis champion.
Jaeger were the first to take
a ski-ing champion's advice
in the matter of a winter
sports wardrobe. And now for
motor clothes — Jaeger lead
in the first lap with this
trim dungaree suit — designed
for Kay Petrie to her ideas
of what a motor-suit should
be. It is made in silk
of many different pastel
colours. In the Sports Shop,
second floor, Jaeger House,
Regent Street.

JAEGER HOUSE, 204-6 REGENT STREET, LONDON, W.1

12   Jaeger advertisement for a dungaree suit,
      Vogue, 15 April 1936
13   Dancers costumed by Coco Chanel in
      Le Train Bleu, premiered by the Ballets Russes,
      Théâtre Champs-Elysées, Paris, 20 June, 1924

13

productional task and an operative system')
by Constructivist designers such as Varvara
Stepanova in Moscow during the 1920s.[22]

Alongside *prozodezhda*, Stepanova was
also committed to the development of
sportodezhda, or garments produced for
competitive and team sports and activities,
which 'were supposed not only to
strengthen the athlete's body but to reinforce
the cohesion of the social body as well'.
Such items 'had to be easy to wear, cut
simply and without buttons… and
identifiable from a distance'. The related
use of distinctive colour allied the resulting
designs both with the striking abstraction
of Constructivist painting and with the
dramatic impact of stage dress, and it is
no coincidence that Stepanova's outfits for
Meyerhold's Modernist theatre functioned
as prototypes 'of a sporting character for
a possible wider use'.[23] They are also
roughly contemporary with the fashion
designer Coco Chanel's iconic costumes
for the 1924 Ballets Russes production of
the Milhaud, Nijinska, Cocteau ballet,
Le Train Bleu. In a famous photograph
of the dancers in bathing, golf and tennis
costumes, the clear elision of sport, the
Modern spirit and Chanel's distinctive
interpretation of sartorial style take us
one step beyond Constructivist theorizing
towards a more tangible glamorization
of sporting endeavour and a parallel
'sportification' of fashion.

The effects of this for the sport and fashion
industries can be found in a continuing
obsession with hygienic design principles
and the reification of sporting talent that
increasingly straddled the blurred boundaries
between the two fields. From the 1920s to

14 Fred Perry in action. c.1934
15 Lacoste tennis dress. French, 1970s.
    V&A: T.586-1995

15

14

the 1970s, tennis witnessed the evolution of a distinctive series of modish looks that migrated from court to catwalk and back, often promoted by specific star players (from Suzanne Lenglen to Bjorn Borg) and always incorporating a clean, precise line that seemed to inscribe current standards of elegance.[24] To cite just two examples: from the 1930s the Englishman Fred Perry brought 'a dash and daring' to the game that translated directly into his sportswear lines when he diversified from professional playing into the manufacture of tennis kit from the late 1940s.[25] In partnership with Austrian footballer Tibby Wegner, he manufactured towelling wristbands before pioneering the crisp honeycomb-weave pique-cotton shirts that cemented the fame of the brand from 1952. Taken up by the subcultural Mod movement in the 1960s, Fred Perry shirts with their tipped sleeves and collars and embroidered laurel-wreath insignia were amongst the first purpose-designed sport garments to migrate into the world of popular street fashion.[26] The foundation of the French sports brand Lacoste was similarly based on the reputation of a tennis player, René Lacoste, a near-contemporary of Perry who won the US Open Championship in 1926 and went on to establish his clothing company with the knitwear manufacturer André Gillier in 1933. From the 1970s the company's products, with their distinctive crocodile badge and pared-down styling, found an appreciative market amongst 'preppy' college students in the United States, a section of society where the cult of physical uniformity continued to enjoy a strong following.[27] The evolutionary trail from *sportodezhda* to the appearance of Lacoste products in Lisa Birnbach's 1980 style bible, *The Official Preppy Handbook*, may have been long and indirect, but in the journey towards the fashion sportswear of the late twentieth century the sartorial language of athleticism finally found a universal context.

PLAY

So far this piece has considered historical examples of the ways in which sporting imperatives and metaphors have influenced the design and promotion of clothing in the wider sphere of fashion. It is also important to identify moments when clothes designed expressly for the performative functions of particular sports have generated an expressive sartorial language of their own – one that, whilst peculiar to the physical requirements of specific games and pursuits, is imbued with a distinctive sense of style and modernity. According to cultural theorist Andrew Blake, this 'sense' equates with historian Johann Huizinga's influential 'characterisation of the human species as homo ludens, the animals who play, [which] illuminates any consideration of sport and leisure more brightly than theories of modernisation'.[28] Blake argues that in order to understand 'the ways in which sports work to transmit pleasure' we need to think of this 'sense' as a branch of aesthetics.

Yet, the underlying design principles applied to many sporting goods often seem to derive from more rationalist, scientific demands. As Blake suggests, 'at one level clothing is crucial to the success of the performer. Ski pants and cycling helmets are designed to increase airspeed through diminished wind-resistance… shoes are made for grip and spin…. There is no doubt that… the redesign of the body which is offered by leading manufacturers can help to improve the performance of a leading athlete. There is equally no doubt that no manufacturer would develop a range of sports goods simply so that they can be worn by a few dozen… successful professionals… Sports goods fulfil one or both of two functions: they help the amateur to play to a high standard, and help those who cannot even hit a ball to identify with the player or team of their choice.'[29] One could argue further that it is in the experience of and participation in the sporting performance, and in the identification with success, that the playfulness of sport finds its main outlets; and that clothing designed to enhance these sensations is a crucial part of the alchemy.

In three of the most popular amateur sports of the nineteenth and twentieth centuries these links between body, performance, costume and fun were highly evident and sometimes quite complex. Cycling, for example, enjoyed a huge popularity in Northern Europe and America during the late 1890s and generated a subculture whose demands and effects were witnessed not just in the production of bicycles, but also in the establishment of social clubs devoted to the sport, the founding of specialist journals and even the promotion of associated leisure activities such as amateur photography.[30] The acceptance of performance-enhancing dress, however, was a little more complic-ated. An article in *Chambers' Journal* of 1894 promoted the health-giving, energizing effects of the sport, particularly for women, suggesting that cycling 'has done more to improve the health of women than almost anything that has been invented. An organically sound woman may cycle with as much impunity as a man. Women are capable of great improvement where the opportunity exists; but their dress handicaps them.'[31] Much has since been written by fashion historians

17   Tennis dress. Machine-sewn white and green
      linen, with mother-of-pearl buckle. Scottish, 1926.
      V&A: T.260-1976

on the way that bloomers (the loose trousers for women promoted from the early 1850s by women's rights advocates and social progressives) found through cycling a route to mass-acceptance and solved the practical reservations expressed in *Chambers'*. But although their presence in advertisements and commentary was ubiquitous, in real life social convention demanded the continued wearing of a skirt over the bifurcated garments, particularly in the company of men.[32] For the time being the pressures of propriety and fashionability won out, although not perhaps at the expense of fun and exhilaration, as a poster promoting Swift Cycles of 1898 makes clear.

Tennis dress for women followed a similar trajectory, where the demands of decorum, comfort, style and pleasure wrestled for prominence until the emergence of a truly rationalized costume after the First World War. On the surface, there is little to connect the exquisite white linen shift dress of around 1926, in the V&A's collection, with its mother-of-pearl buckled belt and inset green squares laid out in Art Deco fashion at neck, hips and skirt-hem, with the cumbersome costumes that passed for tennis wear in the 1870s and '80s (although fashion historian Campbell Warner notes the introduction of pliable knitted jersey and loosely draped 'aesthetic' styles for the game during this period).[33] In terms of construction and 'fit for purpose' they were quite literally generations apart, reflecting both dominant contemporary notions of acceptable feminine appearance and behaviour and also developing styles of play (from the restrained and static game of the nineteenth century to the exuberance

associated with the fashionable French player Suzanne Lenglen in the early 1920s, her costumes styled by the couturier Jean Patou). Yet both also engaged with a sense of modishness that elevated the sport's association with glamour and display above more practical concerns. As the fashion adviser in the magazine *Woman's Life* avowed in 1924: 'My dear ladies, a tennis frock which is the last word in smartness, and which is also the most comfortable model it is possible to have, is a thing to be wished for more than anything at the moment.'[34]

Even more than cycling or tennis, 'the development of clothing for water activities has been intimately connected to modesty standards for women'.[35] The tendency of swimwear to accentuate the lines of the body when wet has also ensured that the swimsuit made the swiftest entry into the hedonistic and erotic registers of twentieth-century fashion, while also retaining a strong association with the Platonic foundations of the idea of sport as a higher spiritual and physical endeavour. In the 1920s and '30s sunbathing, swimming and diving inspired an iconic repertoire of striking images by photographers such as Hoyningen-Heune, in which the knitted costumes of men and women perfectly framed the lithe torsos, exposed tanned limbs and streamlined hair of latter-day Greek deities.[36] Here was a sport/fashion that perfectly captured the liberating and revolutionary potential of 'play' alluded to by contemporary cultural critics such as Wolfgang Graeser, who in his 1927 book *Body Sense, Gymnastics, Dance, Sport* suggested:

Something new has appeared. It could be called a movement, a wave, a fashion, a passion, a new feeling for life; this is a reality that has inundated, pursued, inspired, reformed and influenced millions of people. It had no name but was called by a hundred old names and a hundred new ones... Body culture, gymnastics, dance... the new corporeality... the revival of the ideals of antiquity... The entire Western world and its sphere of influence has been transformed by this strange new sensibility and way of life...[37]

In the twenty-first century, as Christopher Wilk of the V&A attests, 'the legacy of the inter-war healthy body culture is still very much with us', but 'today's health obsessions seem focused on an imagined ideal of immortality. Above all they focus on a model of youthfulness which, many seem to believe, can be achieved through traditional and alternative medical care, cosmetic surgery, exercise and diet. Whereas health was debated by Modernists in terms of a collective ideal... today's body culture is created and consumed on an individual basis.'[38] Here the democratic knitted bathing costume of the 1930s (which often sagged alarmingly when it came into contact with water, regardless of the muscular tone of the body beneath) accedes to the body-hugging potential of Lycra, a synthetic-elastic fabric developed in the late 1950s whose adaptation for sport and then fashion from the 1960s onwards has forever associated its use with the individualistic 'body-conscious culture of self-improvement, body-sculpting and healthy-living' linked to the narcissistic culture of the 1980s and '90s.[39]

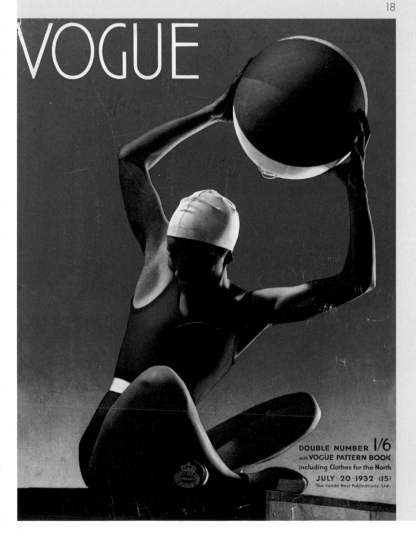

18

20   J. B. Waring, Boxing match between Ben Caunt and
     John Perry (Perry the Black), Wesminster Baths.
     Watercolour on paper, London, 1846. V&A: 809:16

DESIRE

Narcissism and erotic obsession, however, have played an important part in the evolution of modern sport culture since well before the 1980s, often cohering around the figure of the sports star or celebrity and his or her relationship to the fan. It is in this relationship that one of the strongest links between the worlds of fashion and sport resides, but its formation was a gradual affair, only coming to full fruition towards the end of the twentieth century. In late eighteenth-century England, for example, the boxer rose to great heights as a figure of fame and adulation in the dandified world of London Society. One such character, the retired fighter Bob Gregson, was the landlord of the fashionable Castle Tavern in Holborn, and as a commentator of 1810 noted: 'a finer or better proportioned athletic man could not be met with… He was considered by the celebrated professor of Anatomy a most excellent subject to descant upon… He was likewise selected by the late Sir Thomas Lawrence as a fine subject… his general deportment was above all absurd affectation; nothing supercilious was to be found in his manner… he was always well, nay fashionably dressed.'[40]

Besides his personal engagement with the fashionable scene, there were further correspondences between the Regency boxer's muscular physique and the tight 'neo-classical' tailoring adopted by the dandy; and commemorative images of famous boxers were widely disseminated through mass-produced prints and ceramics. Similarly, 'at the close of the nineteenth century, professional footballers were already better known than local MPs, their photographs were displayed in shops, and it was said that "they cannot move in their native streets without receiving ovations enough to turn the head of a Prime Minister"'.[41] But opportunities for a fuller commodification of the successful sportsman through promotional techniques and a close engagement with the workings of the fashion industry did not arise until the beginnings of the age of the celebrity in the post-Second World War era. The phenomenon of celebrity, as sociologist Chris Rojek has famously pointed out, arose as concepts of deference, worship and work changed to reflect a society that was increasingly equal, non-religious and consumerist.[42] In place of the old-style hero, who was defined by action, the celebrity 'is forged through media attention, through the cultivation and projection of image'. The celebrity, as sports-media theorist Barry Smart indicates, 'is superficial, trivial, bereft of distinction, in short insubstantial' and thus more amenable to constant manipulation as a cipher for public desires and aspirations. 'When reference is made to celebrities the emphasis tends to be placed on their marital relations and sexual habits, on their tastes… in drinking, dress, sports cars, and interior decoration…. [in a] desperate effort to distinguish among the indistinguishable.'[43]

Smart is drawing here on historian Daniel Boorstin's work on star-struck American culture in the 1960s, but his comments might just as well be applied to the shifting character of British football in the same era. No other footballing celebrity better symbolizes the changes that were transforming the game during this period than Manchester United player George Best, whose style on and off the pitch set the most powerful precedent for succeeding generations of star players. Besides establishing himself as a sportsman of 'extraordinary flair and colour', Best created a magnetic persona through his endorsement of, and engagement with the fashionable lifestyle of the Swinging Sixties. In 1966 he launched a chain of clothing boutiques in Manchester and on the back of his fame advertised everything from Stylo football boots to Match chewing gum and Fore aftershave.[44] But it was Best's saturnine, hedonistic and sexually-open image that endured longest in the public imagination, paving the way for the contemporary marketing phenomenon that is David Beckham. As Smart concludes: 'high incomes and associated extravagant lifestyles plus the media attention they attract, have transported prominent and successful sporting figures onto another plain, an astral plain.... Sports stars appear in many respects now to be comparable to celebrities from the worlds of film, television and popular music, although the extent and durability of their appeal may be greater. In terms of global popularity or appeal there are now few, if any other professions that can begin to compare to sport.'[45]

As sports historians Richard Holt and Tony Mason astutely observe, before 'the 1950s sport occupied a niche – a massive one perhaps, but still a niche – where as now it is flowing into every nook and cranny of society, refusing to be compartmentalised in the traditional way... Branded sports clothes and shoes like Nike were increasingly universal... Wearing football shirts became common dress... By the end of the [twentieth] century it was commonplace to refer to sport as an "industry" – a term that would have sounded strange to post-war ears when industry still

meant... shipbuilding... Sport had to be promoted as if the product, like jam or jeans, tea or toothpaste, was always at the same level of consistency and quality: fiercely hyped, always thrilling and forever young.'[46] Branding and marketing may be the avenues through which the pure gesture of the sporting hero now achieves 'astral' status, but as Barthes first suggested, an engagement with sport still has the capacity to move the participant and the viewer beyond the realm of the everyday towards the divine, in much the same way that the aspirant dream-world of contemporary fashion promises an escape from the ordinary. It is little wonder then that the two spheres share so much in common, or that their histories and developing interests have constantly overlapped.

21

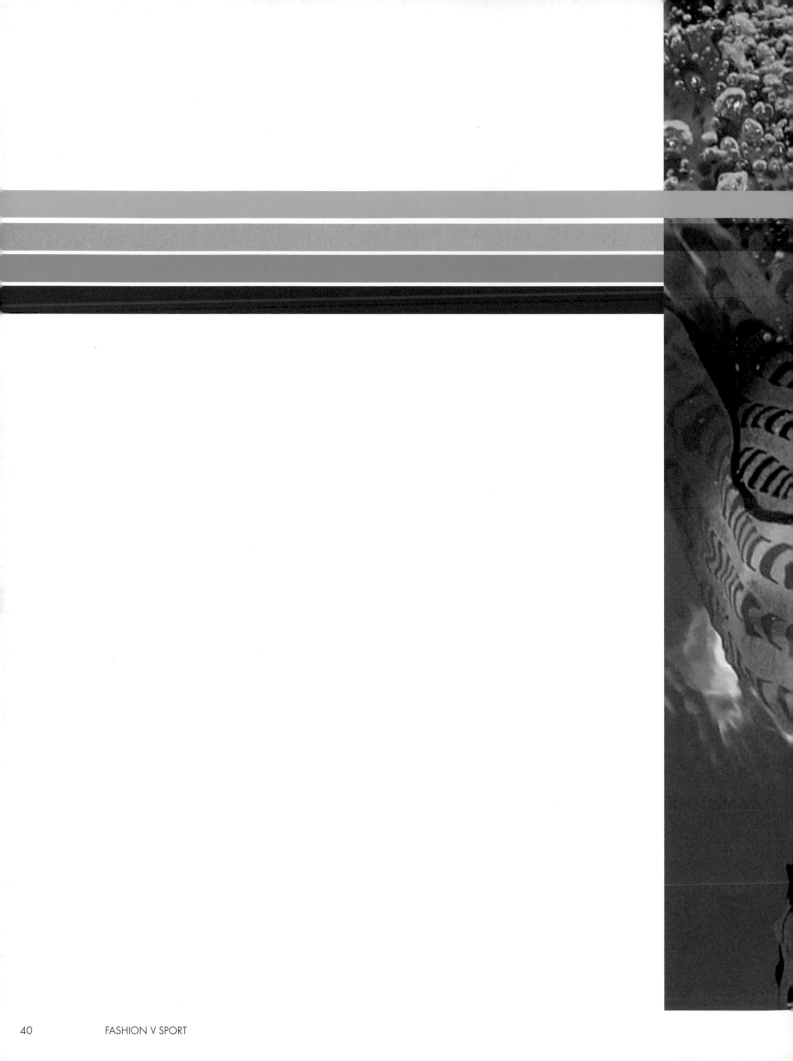

DARE

TRADITION
V
INNOVATION

Although founded primarily on its engagement with the body – both in physical shape and capability – the relationship between fashion and sportswear is characterized by a struggle between tradition and innovation.[1]

Probably the best and most vivid example to illustrate this tussle is the disallowed Puma UniQT all-in-one football kit designed for the Cameroon team for the 2004 African Cup of Nations. Its development began in 2001, and a predecessor featuring sleeveless shirts was worn for the 2002 tournament. It culminated in the 2004 version, a skin-tight all-in-one Lycra-based outfit that allowed for greater freedom of movement, with short-cut silhouette 'shorts', and better breatheability, with layers of micromesh in the 'shirt'. Even though the kit retained the look of a traditional football outfit, with separate colours for the top and bottom, its innovatory nature led to its disqualification. Fifa President Sepp Blatter maintained that it went 'against the laws of the game. The rules are very clear, there is one shirt, one shorts and one socks [sic]'. He went on to proclaim that Fifa 'are the guardians of the laws of the game – the laws are universal'.[2] The subsequent disallowal of the kit was not only a drawback for the Cameroon team – Puma also filed a legal case against Fifa. The incident highlights the inherent contradiction facing many traditional team sports as well as games such as tennis.

Most individual sports, such as cycling, running and swimming, where the primary concern regarding clothing is with function and performance, do not appear to have encountered such difficulties, as the popularity of Speedo's Fastskin swimming suits highlights. Its combination of a smoother and more flexible fabric for the upper body and a fabric that 'mimics the rough shark denticles to reduce drag along key areas of the body' apparently 'increases speed by reducing passive drag by up to 4%'.[3] In this case, the four years of research preceding its launch in 2004 proved worthwhile both in terms of performance and profit, since most swimmers have taken up wearing at least one version of this innovative product.

Both these examples demonstrate the amount of time and money sportswear companies invest researching performance-enhancing innovations. The majority is very specific to the type of sport focused on, but much of it could find good use in everyday life. Throughout the history of fashion, only very few designers have made use of these innovations within their designs, but now, due to the speed with which these advances are being made, more fashion designers are beginning to integrate them into their designs. Most prominently, Prada launched their Prada Sport diffusion line (now called 'Prada Linea Rossa') in 1998, while recent collaborations include Comme des Garçons' continuing work with Northface and Speedo.

An interesting case in which both fashion and sport design techniques seem to coexist happily is the Japanese fashion label Visvim, whose creative director Hiroki Nakamura not only has years of experience in the field, working for Snowboard manufacturer Burton before he launched his own label in early 2000, but also has a personal passion for sports. This is most tangible in his approach

23

Previous pages
22 Matt Walsh at the launch of the Speedo Fastskin
    FSII, Sydney 2004. Photograph by Rob Griffith

23 Speedo Fastskin FSII. Technical detail
24 Visvim. Navy Lieutenant coat. Hand woven
    Harris Tweed wool laminated with Gore-tex.
    Autumn/Winter 2006–7
25 Visvim Navy Lieutenant coat. Detail, inside
    Gore-tex taping

24

25

to design, which places great importance on researching the best performing materials for his designs rather than on producing a large number of new designs each season. For example, his continuing close work with Gore-tex has meant that most of the jackets he produces are waterproofed and breatheable without looking like performance sportswear, as his traditional navy pea coat demonstrates. It is here where sports innovation and technology are integrated in the design process and rendered fashionable that the relationship between fashion and sport seems to sit most comfortably and perform at its best.

The 'in-conversation' between Kim Jones, a British menswear designer and collaborator with Umbro, and Suzanne Lee, Senior Research Fellow at Central Saint Martins and author of the book *Fashioning the Future: Tomorrow's Wardrobe*, which features in this section of the book, explores his experience and ideas regarding the differing design methods used in fashion and sport, and sheds light on some of the challenges and opportunities of the collaborative process.

SUZANNE LEE AND KIM JONES

IN-CONVERSATION

Suzanne Lee, Senior Research Fellow at Central Saint Martins College of Art and Design, interviews Kim Jones, British menswear designer and collaborator with Umbro.

SL How would you describe your approach to fashion? What are your interests and passions?

KJ Ever since I was about 12 or so and my sister was studying fashion, I would always get passed down *i-D* and *The Face*. I was intrigued by what was happening in these magazines. Coming from such a different world, I was just really excited by what the magazines showed and I realized I wanted to work in the creative field, but I did not know exactly where. I started out doing graphics and photography in my foundation course and then I did a degree at Camberwell College of Arts, which was a bit boring. It seemed to be a lot of middle-aged women going back just to do a hobby. There were a few of us who reacted against that and started doing bits and pieces of freelancing and working whilst at college. It was always around fashion, whether it was doing fashion photography or graphics for a T-shirt company. After I graduated, for a couple of years I was doing photography and freelancing, but I just did not like working and travelling around that much. I wanted to be more settled and decided to do design, because I had always been interested in clothes. It also allowed me to bring everything together, which is what I can do now: some photography, some styling, art direction, as well as designing. So I did a portfolio and went to Central Saint Martins to be interviewed, where I was told that I did not need another degree and could do it on my own. I wanted to do the degree, because I wanted to have the time to find out exactly which area I like, and what I want to do. As I have always collected

29

clothes and shoes, I began by drawing from my collections. By now it has developed into something of its own, because from being referential what I do now is completely non-referential. My pieces are trying to push things forward by mixing street and fashion.

SL   Your work references sport a lot. Have you ever had an interest in sport?

KJ   Not really. I used to cycle five miles a day and run five miles a day, up until about the age of 19. The kinds of sports I like are more solitary rather than team sports. But generally I am not that interested in sport. I like sportswear, but 'sportswear' is such a loose term. You look at sportswear from America, from the 1950s onwards, and you look at James Dean – you realize that a T-shirt is sportswear. Or a pair of jeans is sportswear. I suppose I prefer the casual side of dressing rather than dressing up, because I think it is much more relevant to menswear. I like to see people dressing up, but I feel it is not relevant in my world or the world of the people I know, so I try to focus on the area that I think is relevant.

SL   This is true. The idea of informality fashioned through the introduction of sportswear is certainly something that is going to come across in the Fashion V Sport exhibition. Is that something you think is here to stay?

KJ   I cannot really see a sudden reversion back to suits. Especially when you look at the Spring/Summer 2007 collections, such as Prada and Missoni – everyone's doing it. It is that mixing up of things, and this is happening all over the

world. I have been to Australia and Hawaii recently, and everyone is merging into one thing. I think that is due to the internet. That seems to be the reason – and the way forward – because everyone has the information so quickly they are able to mix it into their own style. I like the fact that everyone has their own unique style, but in an 'en masse' way.

SL   When you use the term 'sportswear' now, what does that mean to you?

KJ   I do not think of it as sportswear, I think of it as casual wear. But 'sportswear' is the terminology for it. If you go back, from the 1940s, 1950s, 1960s, it has always been much more of an American thing. That is the reason why I showed in New York – because it is a much more American look than it is a European one. We have become really popular in America because of this, and I think it is also because it is much more of a mass-market thing. Fashion nowadays is really high-end, but I think you have to be an established designer like Louis Vuitton to be able to have those prices and justify them, otherwise you have to be mass-market. It is very divided and it will get even more divided. What is important is the way people mix it together.

SL   You have been collaborating with the sportswear company Umbro for several years. How did the collaboration come about?

KJ   After I left college, I got a lot of press with Dazed and Confused and The Face, and my PR at the time got a call from someone that worked for Vans, because I had used them in a shoot. They were also

32

31

doing the PR for Umbro and said that they were looking for someone to consult them. I began by doing a vintage line for them, looking through their archive and reworking it. It was really small to begin with and as I got more press, they became more interested in me and asked me to do a line of my own for them. The challenge for me was that they were not perceived as a very cool brand, at least in Britain. It is funny, because in Italy and in America they are, but in mainland Europe and northern Europe they are not. In Japan Umbro is the third biggest selling brand in sportswear.

SL How does your relationship with them work? Do they give you a completely free brief or do they set parameters?

KJ They give you a rough line sheet of how many styles we are going to do. They have never turned round and said no to anything. But then there are some things like the platform trainers we did, which were a real press piece, but they would not produce them to sell. This was a shame, because we get a lot of enquiries through the website. Umbro could have placed them in Colette in Paris or Dover Street Market in London; they do not realize how the high end trickles down.

SL So is that perhaps a point of tension? Where it is too 'pure fashion', and it has moved too far away from the sport function, to the point where they just do not get it anymore?

KJ I believe that this experience was important. They trust me on things like that now. When I do certain designs they can be opposed to them at first, but then they

see them in the flesh – for example, the see-through tracksuit that we did in the first season – and then they usually like them.

SL I am quite interested in the limitations of the collaboration process. Is it only in footwear when they stop you, and tell you that they cannot produce it?

KJ Well, the apparel was actually the bigger seller, rather than the footwear. I think it was something like 70:30 per cent. I treated the apparel line very much as a diffusion from my own line. So I took some of the designs through from my previous season, so the collaboration products become almost like a streetwear label. I wanted it to be something that is really approachable for the kind of guys that model for me, because they are a very specific kind of guy, a good-looking but really regular guy. They are a good gauge of how things are going, because they might not be your customers for Kim Jones, but they are your customers for Umbro by Kim Jones.

SL I wondered whether there was a crossover in your customer? Would the Umbro-Kim Jones buyer also be someone who would buy into your main line?

KJ I think they would, eventually, because the tailoring aspects of what we do would start to have more appeal. I want the main line to be something where people who really love clothes go and buy Kim Jones, but then people that really like to just feel comfortable and wear nice clothes buy Umbro by Kim Jones. I want it to be something where lots of people can wear it and feel cool in it.

SL You say you began the Umbro collaboration by diffusing what you had done for your previous collection for Kim Jones and feeding that in?

KJ Yes, but there are also some of the more sporty things that I would not necessarily put into my line. I look at some stuff, and think I really like that and that would work really well, but I cannot do it for Kim Jones, so I'll do it for Umbro by Kim Jones.

SL So is that a two-way transfer? When you're researching, having access to an archive anywhere is quite inspiring. Were there any discoveries in the Umbro archive that influenced your main line, or that you kept to one side to filter into your own line later on?

KJ Actually there were not in that instance.

SL When you are researching, are you inspired by fabrics or by a certain technique? Does sportswear, specifically its materials, styling or technical aspects, feed directly into your design process and collections?

KJ I do love the technical aspect of sportswear and in the last few collections I have worked on with Umbro, they have had a technical designer who worked with me. This has been really interesting, because I have learned a lot of things I had not come across before. They were showing me new techniques, different ways of bonding fabrics and sealing things, and lightweight packable fabrics that allow you to make a tiny little ball out of a jacket. Things I had never come across. You do not have time to explore all those things

34 Niyi in Adicolor black series, Keith Haring and Jeremy
    Scott suit pants, 2006. Photograph by Paul Hartnett
35 Y-3, Autumn/Winter 2006–7

as a fashion designer. It is a very specific area with a very specific knowledge base. That is why a sportswear designer is a sportswear designer, and a fashion designer is a fashion designer.

SL You must now see yourself as transgressing some of those boundaries, since you have begun to acquire some of the knowledge that perhaps a technical designer has?

KJ Yes, but then the sportswear industry spends so much money on technological research like that, so unless you have constant contact with it, you fall behind very quickly. You see how much money they put into making one football boot, using all these crazy materials such as titanium and fabrics that are woven up, and you think that it is crazy to spend that much only to make it a tiny bit lighter. I still find that quite questionable.

SL I guess to a certain extent they have to justify new products.

KJ Yes, as they spend a fortune, many millions of pounds, developing it.

SL Do Umbro see themselves as leading the technical side of things? Where do they position themselves?

KJ I am not really sure. I think they are trying to find ways of prolonging the interest in their company, whether through technology or through trend apparel. The sportswear market is so competitive, much more competitive than the fashion market, because you can define much more of an identity with a fashion brand. But with

a sportswear brand, you can take two jackets, take the labels off and you would not know who had made them. A lot of companies, such as Adidas and Nike, are looking back at their history. This is not necessarily bringing design forward, but the way that they are reappropriating what they did in the past with new techniques makes it exciting – like Adidas collaborating with Jeremy Scott using Keith Haring's work. I sometimes think it is really good for those companies to look back to enable them to move forward, though not everyone thinks that way.

SL How do you think the fashion industry as a whole perceives these collaborations?

KJ I believe they see them very much in a financial way. I think it is really nice when people collaborate, and there have been some very successful collaborations, like Stella McCartney for Adidas and Alexander McQueen for Puma. And you look at someone like Neil Barrett, who is doing 96 Hours for Puma, which is very much a whole brand. What I wonder sometimes with companies like Puma, who are doing all these collaborations with so many different designers, is when the saturation point will be reached. But then you have Y-3, which was, I think, the fastest growing fashion label ever set up. This shows that it is very much a new way of making money for the fashion industry. But it is also interesting to look at the way that sportswear is now infiltrating into mainstream fashion: those collaborations only really began when I started at Umbro, and now you look at the high street, and you look at sportswear, and it is really leading a lot of men's fashion. It has been

such a rapid process considering I graduated only six years ago, but it has changed so much. Probably about 50 per cent of most men's collections now are either denim or sportswear-based products.

SL   So do you think that what were distinct industries or design genres – fashion and sport – have been eroded for good?

KJ   Yes, but I think this is very much to do with the internet, because people are seeing all the information straight away, and it is just natural for things to merge. You are not going to wear a pair of smart shoes every day, because it is not comfortable, you are going to wear a pair of trainers, and if you are at home, nine times out of ten, at the weekend you might put some tracksuit bottoms on rather than just a pair of jeans. So, essentially it is just the way people are redefining the way they dress.

SL   Do you think it's the industry reacting to the consumer? Or is it just a natural crossover?

KJ   I cannot really tell – the change has happened quite quickly, so it's hard to judge. Obviously the industry is spending millions of pounds finding out what the consumer wants.

SL   They must surely be researching, in terms of most people's wardrobes, what percentage of time, say, or how often, people are wearing trainers as shoes, tracksuit bottoms as trousers. Most people's wardrobes seem to be made up from items originating in sportswear.

KJ   When you look at the catwalk of major fashion houses, 90 per cent of that will not go into a store, so it is not reality, it is what the designer wants to project. If you go into a Louis Vuitton store, they will have all their dress shoes next to a massive selection of trainers. It is 'on trend', and I think it is going to evolve even more. Definitely through the fabrics rather than through the cuts, because the cuts are not going to change that much. It will probably be the innovations in sportswear fabrics and techniques that will become part of fashion more and more, because it is the only way you can bring it forward.

SL   When you sit down to do the Umbro designs, do you have a global picture in your mind?

KJ   I just think very much of youth, but then it crosses over to the age range of people who buy into Kim Jones for Umbro, who are between 16 and 40.

SL   You must notice on your travels what happens when your garments are worn outside the UK. Do people style them differently, or reinterpret them?

KJ   I think because of the internet that happens less and less, because I was in Australia and the kids wear exactly the same clothes as in London, and they look exactly the same as the kids in London. They just sound different.

SL   So you do not believe that there are still quite pronounced local differences?

KJ   Not really.

38

37 Jean Paul Gaultier, Spring/Summer 1990
38 Umbro by Kim Jones, powder-blue low runner,
   fully concealed seams, 2007

SL Do you think, overall, that the future of fashion and the future of sportswear will continue to converge? Do you see it as a moment in time, or is it that things will never be the same again?

KJ I think it is here to stay, just because it is the way people like to dress. But I do not necessarily know what it will be like in ten years, because when you look back at the 1990s it is horrific. So people might look back over what we are doing now and think it is awful. Interestingly, lots of people are looking at Azzedine Alaïa and Comme des Garçons, all things from around 1990 – most of which was quite sports-based, especially when you look at Junior Gaultier. The convergence of fashion and sport has probably always been there, but much more underlying.

SL I think you mentioned it earlier – that fabric innovations were what changed it in the first place.

KJ Indeed, different seaming on footwear, which we did with Umbro: closed seams with no overstitching, which had not been done on that kind of shoe before. Those things you do not really think about. I am not trying to develop techniques or anything like that, but we are just trying, as such a young brand, to hone our identity so it becomes a recognizable thing. So I have been very fortunate with the number of different kinds of companies I have worked with, whether it's been high-end, with Louis Vuitton, Hugo Boss and Mulberry, or sports and high street, with Umbro or Top Man. You learn a different thing from each, so I think it is having those diverse

experiences that has helped me to bring it all together.

SL I have this theory that big, global events also have an impact, whether it is conscious or unconscious, on what is going on in design. So, for example, now we have the 2008 Beijing Olympics coming up and the 2012 Olympics happening in London, the focus, in life, everywhere you look, is going to be on athleticism and performance kit. Whether you are into it or not, it will be permeating everything in our daily lives. I wonder whether there might be a backlash post-Olympics, where everyone is so completely tired of everything to do with sport that suddenly people bring back starched collars, or just more formal, restrictive clothing.

KJ Maybe in 'fashion' terms, but I do not think it would be a 'mass' thing... you have to look at how much people can afford to spend on clothes. And I do not think Top Man would be making starched collars.

SL One thing that I wanted to ask you in terms of the fashion and sport relationship is how you see the difference between menswear and womenswear in relation to it.

KJ It is funny; I think fewer people tap into it in womenswear. You look at Balenciaga and his amazing collection recently where he did the nylon multicoloured zipped garments. I really loved the way that Nicolas Ghesquière used all the nylons and fabrics in a non-sporty way. It was not meant to be a sports thing, it was just

39 Balenciaga, Autumn/Winter 2003
40 Gabrielle, Thiago and Dennis backstage, Kim Jones
    'Sing Sing Sing' collection Spring/Summer 2007,
    Paris. Photograph by Tomoki Sukezane

using those fabrics and making them look really beautiful. I think that is much more the way that womenswear seems to approach it, but there are very few designers in womenswear who use the sportswear fabrics in a way that I like, or who try and make it sporty. It seems to be very half-heartedly thought out.

SL It seems to me that the relationship between womenswear and sports is quite difficult, which is probably to do with its association with masculinity and strength.

KJ Yes. Comme des Garçons do it well, for example, but then they have worked with Northface and Speedo, amongst others. But sometimes I think, why do it yourself, when someone else knows how to do it perfectly? Go and ask them to do it with you.

SL Which leads to another question regarding the status of the sports industry in relation to the fashion industry. One of the things that you mentioned is that sports companies put a lot of time and money into research. Can the crossover between fashion and sport in that sense ever be total?

KJ I care about the performance in fabric – things like silver in fabric to clean it – but it costs so much money. It would cost me much more to buy a fabric like that than it would Nike. So, in effect, unless you are as big a company as that, I do not think the impact necessarily comes through. I always wear sports jackets by someone like Nike, rather than by a designer. I would rather buy the real thing than

a designer copy, because you know that you are going to get better wear out of it, and it is also probably a third of the price. A terrible thing for me to say, but it is true. I never try to emulate a sports thing in my work. Rather I look at someone like a skier, and like the way they look in what they are wearing, and then I take that element into what I do, rather than trying to emulate what it is. In the end I think it is the feeling of sportswear I like more than the product. But the sportswear product itself is great, and its technology and innovation impossible to keep up with.

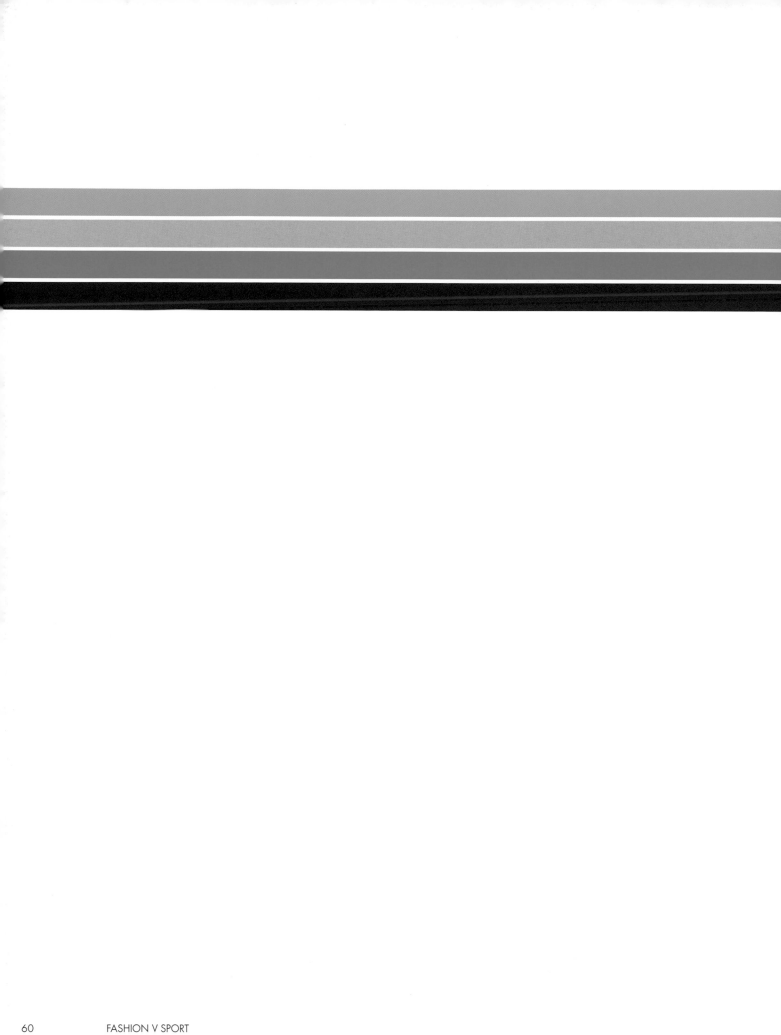

DISPLAY

42

UNIFORMITY
V
INDIVIDUALITY

Sportswear or sports-inspired fashion is often seen to be the most uniform mode of dress, not least when it is worn in allegiance to a team: but also because its focus lies ostensibly on practicality and comfort rather than style and cut. There is nothing more ubiquitous than a pair of trainers, a hooded jersey top and a pair of tracksuit bottoms, yet strangely this has become one of the most diversified and specialized areas of design in terms of the quantity of varied product available to the consumer.

This is often seen in relation to the dubious possibility, produced by consumer capitalism, of creating a sense of individuality through clothes. As philosopher Kate Scoper laments:

High-street fashion may offer the individual a kind of way of belonging, but only in the pseudo-mode of the serial collective – in the ode of the market itself, which flourishes on constantly renewed ways of providing essentially homogenous forms of consumption rather than on promoting genuine difference and eccentricity.[1]

Philosopher Gilles Lipovetsky's view of the possibilities of expressing individuality through dress is less bleak. He interprets the 'preference for casual clothing' as a 'new age of individualism', believing that 'the vogue for sportswear reflects, in the sphere of dress, the demand for greater personal freedom; this freedom is reflected in fashion, in turn, by casualness, the relaxed look, flexibility and humorous decorations and inscriptions'.[2]

43

44

These diverging opinions on the options sports-inspired clothes offer the individual only highlight the innate conflict in the relationship between fashion and sport, as what sportswear does, to a certain extent, is to erase difference in status and wealth, when traditionally one of the main functions of clothes was to establish it. Sports-inspired clothes also seem to make it considerably more difficult to indicate belonging to a particular social group due to their inconspicuous appearance. However, this does not mean that nowadays everyone looks the same. As Sophie Woodward carefully analyses here, in her essay 'Standing out as one of the crowd', the knowledge of subtle alterations or differences seems to be the key to understanding the way that sportswear is worn.

Examples of this are plentiful, but most obvious in the various ways individuals customize their clothes. Whether these are home-made changes – how laces are tied, how caps are worn – or more professionally personalized products, such as the individually hand-engraved trainers British designer I Saw makes, or indeed the reassembled and redesigned sports jackets and T-shirts fashion label Dr. Romanelli produces, they indicate a desire and need for individualization of what appears on the surface to be a homogenous mass of inexpensively produced apparel and shoes.

This has, of course, already been picked up and catered for by sportswear brands through various customization services: for example, the aforementioned Reebok Rbk custom service allows you to personalize a variety of shoes by choosing colour and material, while the more ethically minded

Puma's Top Winner Thrift initiative invited people to an exhibition of 510 pairs of trainers, each individually put together from recycled clothes.

The professionalizing of customization does not, however, dampen 'the originality of the process that is under way', which, as Lipovetsky explains, 'lies precisely here: the progressive, undeniable tendency toward the reduction of extremes does not culminate in the unification of appearances, but in a subtle differentiation'.[3] The street, as a platform to perform this 'subtle differentiation', therefore becomes the most crucial space for the convergence of fashion and sport.

STANDING OUT AS ONE OF THE CROWD

SOPHIE WOODWARD

There is no more striking evidence of the uniformity of sportswear than the sight of thousands of football fans clad in identical replica kits as a sign of allegiance to their team. This uniformity is no less apparent, albeit in a less explicit way, in everyday clothing choices: items of sportswear, such as trainers, hoodies and tracksuits, have become ubiquitous as part of the uniform of youth. Yet the functionality or practicality of sportswear is only one concern people have when choosing to dress this way, for sportswear forms part of the everyday performance of identity, staged not on playing fields but in the streets, clubs and bars of the city.

Identity as expressed through clothing emerges through the relationship between the individual and particular social groups, and what is at stake is credibility, belonging and standing out. It may be articulated through a desire both for sameness, to 'fit in', and for differentiation, since self-identity comes through an understanding of being different from others.[1] As the sociologist Georg Simmel has argued, the tension between the desire to be part of a social group and the 'individual elevation from it' is a core dynamic of being human,[2] and in turn this is central to the propulsion of fashion change. It is as much a dynamic of the fashion system as it is of the individual, as he or she chooses what to wear on a daily basis.

This essay will consider this dynamic in relation to the everyday wearing of sportswear, based upon a research project entitled 'Fashionmap' – a mass observation of street fashion in Nottingham[3] – and qualitative interviews carried out in London.

It is undeniable that the omnipresence of such items as trainers and hoodies in the streets and bars of Britain has made sportswear a 'uniform of youth'. However, inasmuch as wearing a claret and blue football shirt rather than a red and white one is a matter of immense importance, so too is the choice of a particular brand or style that allows the individual to fit into particular groups or localized identities. Ironically, choosing items that are apparently uniform is also an act of differentiation. This essay will also address how individuals are able to find a space for difference within these shared sartorial codes of belonging through (often subtle) markers. The tensions that emerge are those between uniformity and differentiation, where individualization also involves subverting or contesting the implicit masculinity of sportswear,[4] since through customization a more ambiguous gendered identity can be constructed.

46   Young man in a tracksuit and cap, standing
     with his sister, Nottingham
47   Young man in a hoodie, Nottingham

INVISIBLE
UNIFORMITY

According to one young man, who was interviewed in Nottingham wearing trainers, jeans, a hoodie and a cap, he dresses to 'fit in with everyone else', his main aim being 'just to look normal'. Since so many items of sportswear have come to dominate the everyday dress of young people, wearing them is a means for them to blend in. Sportswear forms an example of an 'informal uniform',[5] which when adopted can alleviate anxiety or concern about 'getting it wrong'. The informal uniform may not be subject to explicit rules or regulations, yet the social censure of peer groups acts as a source of regulation. The wearing of sportswear in this way, as a form of invisible uniformity, runs counter to the notion that in the absence of explicit regulations, people choose clothing to assert their individuality.[6] Instead, this absence of clear rules is a cause of anxiety; by choosing uniform items such as sportswear, and perhaps to an even greater degree denim jeans, a person is allowed to become part of the invisible majority.

In order to avoid social censure, what matters is not only the wearing of particular brands, but also the way in which these items are worn, which has to look completely natural in terms of walk, movement and bodily stance. An overview of the images collected as part of the Fashionmap project in Nottingham shows a sameness in the stance of those who were photographed in sportswear, as they stood with their hands in their pockets, the whole body loosened in a relaxed pose (Plate 45). This stance is created both by the informality and lack of structure of the sportswear clothing (mostly baggy and loose), and also by cultural expectation, as they demonstrate their basic competences in wearing the clothing.

Since the majority of people that were photographed in sportswear were men, this underlines the implicit masculinity of sportswear, for 'male sports clothing is normative of modern masculinity'.[7] This applies as much to the male stance and wearing of sportswear as it does to the choices made by the women photographed. A clear trend that emerged from the images collected was that few women wore top-to-toe tracksuits (other than those of school age), whereas many men did (Plate 46). Women tended to wear trainers, and perhaps a hoodie, yet often with fitted jeans, and as the woman in Plate 46 shows, these are often low-slung to display their flesh. The man wears the characteristic top-to-toe baggy tracksuit, and as he stands next to her, their respective femininity and masculinity are emphasized. In both pictures, there is still an evident attempt by the men to differentiate themselves through the way they wear their hats. In one case, the cap is perched on the top of the head, at a side angle, and in another, a stretch hat is worn almost pulled off the back of the head. In both instances, neither is overtly questioning the implicit masculinity or norms of sportswear, but they are nevertheless able to find space for individual manoeuvre within this.

46

DIFFERENTIATED
UNIFORMITY

49

Whilst for some, sportswear allows them
to remain unnoticed among the mass of
people wearing trainers and tracksuit tops,
for others it is a means simultaneously to
differentiate themselves from this mass,
and to align themselves with a particular
group of people and shared identity. In
some instances this happens at the micro-
level, as small groups of friends find their
individual styles converging around a shared
'look'. The two young men in Plates 47
and 48 are friends, and were stopped and
photographed together. At a superficial
glance, their clothing does not stand out
as unusual – both are wearing trainers and
tracksuits in colours that are typical of many
of those we photographed (grey and navy).
However, the marker of difference is the kind
of knitted hat they are both wearing; the hat
is identical, and when asked about it, they
state that it was not something that their other
friends wear, although one of the young
men's cousins has the same hat. Although
this marker of difference is shared by these
men, they then articulate their uniqueness
by wearing the hat in different ways, as one
of them wears it underneath his hoodie, with
only the bobbles at the side being visible
(Plate 47), while the other wears it fully
visible. The 'individuality' they are const
ructing is not to make them 'incomparable'[8]
to others by standing out from the crowd
completely. Nor does this individuality rely
upon them being autonomous and divorced
from the ties of other people; instead they
use clothing to make connections to their
friend, and the other young man (the cousin).
It is through the position of a hood or a hat
that they personalize their outfit.

In many instances, this notion of a shared
identity is focused upon specific sites in the

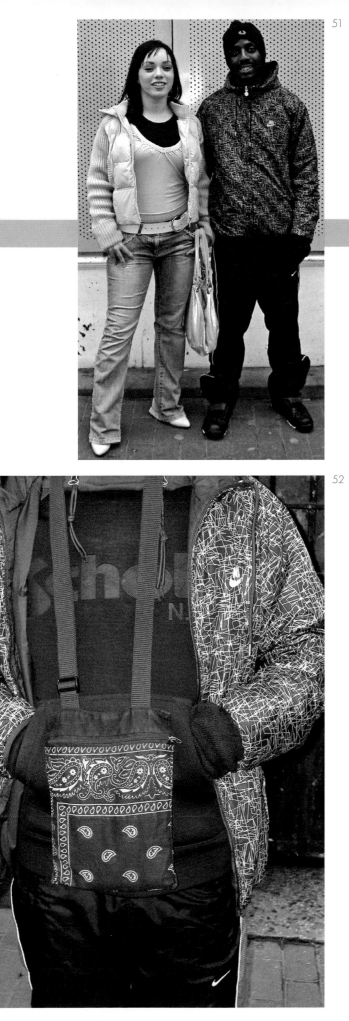

51

50 Young man's friend in a matching hat
    and Y-3 tracksuit, Nottingham
51 Young man and his girlfriend, Nottingham
52 Young man's money pouch

45–52 Photographs by Claire Murphy

52

city; in some cases it is concentrated on particular bars and streets, but in others it is about marking allegiance to an area. The young man in Plate 51 is an example of someone who again, at first glance, does not look particularly distinctive, in that he is wearing trainers and a dark blue Nike tracksuit. He loves the top, which is reversible – a fact that he feels makes him stand out slightly, since he has not seen anyone else wearing it. Underneath his jacket is the pouch that he carries his money in (Plate 52); this was made by his friends, and is something that the majority of the people in his 'group' wear. According to the young man, the trend started in London, but now the pouch is being made in Nottingham, it has been adapted and made particular to the area. He marks his friendship group in a subtle (and often concealed) manner, as it forms part of his group's shared code of belonging. He also owns a hat with 'NG3' on it, which he bought from a shop and had especially customized for him. 'NG3' is the postcode of the St Ann's area of Nottingham where he lives, a district that has also acquired a certain notoriety since it is associated with gang culture. The hat is, in contrast, not something that those from his group or area wear, and as such, when he wears it, he is using territory to construct an individual identity. He chose it because, despite the bad press the area often gets, he says he is 'happy where I'm from', and he challenges the district's negative image with the construction of a positive marker of identity.

Whilst the hat is an explicit marker of the area with which the young man identifies, in contrast, the pouch involves an understated code of belonging.

53

PERSONALIZING UNIFORMS

54

There is a clear tension in almost everyone interviewed between needing to fit in to a particular group, and wanting to find some space for creating an outfit that fitted with their own personal aesthetic.[9] One young man interviewed in London had grown up in Cambridge, but always had a strong sense of being different. He both felt and looked unlike those he was at school with, yet was not necessarily comfortable standing out alone. Once he started working in a shop specializing in streetwear he found a niche of people who were different from the Cambridge mainstream. He started going down to East London at the weekends with this group, and for the last year he has lived and worked there. He states that more than anything he dresses to 'fit in' to this scene, although he has developed a very clearly personalized style of dressing. He observes that even though there is a wide range of styles worn in East London, there is still a degree of uniformity in what people wear. This 'uniformity' is fluid enough to allow individualized looks to proliferate, yet is still sufficiently identifiable for individuals to know what they are trying to 'fit in' to.

The outfit the young man is wearing is typical of his style, which is the same when he works or goes out. Much of his current clothing is determined by what he can afford, and as he works in Covent Garden's Maharishi streetwear store, he owns many items from there (in particular their diffusion range, which is more of a streetwear style). Now that he lives in East London his style has become much more set, only evolving gradually. This is mostly the case with his trousers, which mirror his current interest in cut and design (he is presently setting up his own streetwear label). Rather than attaching himself to external brands, his style of trousers evolves out of what he previously wore. When he was younger he was very brand-conscious, and displayed the label; his move away from this reinforces the association of sportswear with youth, as the young people (under 21) photographed tended to wear labels in an obvious way. Much as the American economist Thorstein Veblen argued that fashion in the early twentieth century was an 'index of the wealth of its wearer',[10] in the case of twenty-first-century sportswear, brand labels – for teenagers – can be seen as an 'index' of status, coolness and fitting in.

This man exemplifies the complex interrelationship between 'fitting in' and 'standing out'; he wants to fit in to the East London scene and the music scene (he works as a DJ, playing mostly electro music, or going to New Rave parties). In many ways he mirrors the attitudes of many interviewed, since they primarily dressed to fit in, yet wanted a degree of personalization and customization in their outfit. His boss (and close friend) dresses in a similar way to him, which is rarely a problem unless, as on one occasion, they wear an 'uncomfortably similar' outfit. For many of the people in the Nottingham sample, personalization of dress was achieved through detailing, exemplifying what philosopher Gilles Lipovetsky terms 'marginal differentiation': new fashion styles differing from previous ones only in terms of small changes in cut, style or access-orization. One young man, dressed in a grey hoodie, grey cap, white trainers and a pair of jeans, was wearing five rings (of skulls), and had two keyrings, one of

a Chupa Chups lolly, and the other of a little bird. Through these details, he was able to introduce a tension in his outfit between the implicit masculinity of the sportswear, the explicitness of the rings and the contradictory playfulness of the keyrings. Others managed this by wearing unusual-coloured trainers, adding their own laces to shoes or personalizing accessories.

55–56 Young woman in a gold-chain graphic T-shirt
and Nike Air Force 1 trainers (detail page 77).
Photograph by STYLESNIPER

MANAGING CONTRADICTIONS

55

A young woman interviewed in London
has a history of wearing sportswear that
is even more markedly characterized by
contradictions. She is now 27; when she
was younger her wardrobe had two very
different sides: one full of feminine, playful
dresses, and the other linked to sportswear –
first house-music and later hip-hop inspired.
Although her clothing choices were influenced
by the music scene, they were also
determined by the fact that she played
a great deal of sport. In addition to this,
her mother was frequently sewing and
knitting outfits for her, which inspired her
from a young age to make her own
clothing, and desire unique, customized
garments. She still wears sportswear, yet
now she clearly states her frustration with
the fact that it is hard to make it look
feminine. This was not a significant concern
for her until a few years ago, after she had
graduated, since even when she was
studying fashion at Kingston, she tended
to wear big baggy jeans, baggy T-shirts,
caps and trainers – her desire to look more
feminine found expression through the
dresses. Now, she wants this aspect to be
part of an everyday look. She feels she is
'too old' just to wear baggy sports clothing,
and also wants to look more feminine.
This is evident in the clothing she has started
to design (a coming together of craft with
streetwear) as well as in what she wears
and how she looks: her white-blond dyed
hair and red lips display vintage and retro
influences, while her earrings are quite 'Salt-
N-Pepa inspired' – a key influence
in her youth. She still wants to look
fashionable (wearing shorts and leggings).
Her outfit is therefore a mixture of
sportswear, vintage and current fashion,
yet all are articulated through her own

SPRINKLER
STOP VALVE
INSIDE

biography and past as well as personal aesthetic (as she printed the T-shirt herself).

Although the young woman has a clear 'look' – about which she is very particular – she admits that she is most concerned about 'fitting in'; her social life in London revolves around many different social and music scenes, in which she does not ever want to stand out too much. Nor, however, does she simply want to blend in, since she dresses to be noticed. The vintage items that individualize and feminize the sportswear help her achieve this. Her friend jokily refers to her style as 'ragga-retro', which succinctly encapsulates the ways in which she is able to create a coherent, if contradictory, look.

In a unique way, this young woman still exemplifies the concerns everyone interviewed had about both standing out and fitting in. This concern is a core dynamic of everyday clothing choices,[12] yet acquires a particular resonance in the case of sportswear, which is both implicitly masculinized and, when worn alone, difficult to 'stand out' in. What becomes apparent when considering why and how people put their outfits together is that this seeming uniformity hides many complex, overlapping dynamics. This demonstrates the tension Simmel identified as common to all people,[13] between being an accepted part of a social group and being elevated from it.[14] For him, what differentiates social and sartorial types (such as the bohemian, or the dandy) is the balance between these two factors. So it is in the case of sportswear: some adopt it to be 'unseen', others to align themselves to a group or to develop a personal style. In each case, the variant is the relative emphasis upon

blending in or becoming distinctive. Sportswear as everyday dress can be understood as a manifestation of the tension between uniformity and individuality, rather than as a defined categorization of types, where some are designated as 'individuals' and others as 'conformists'. It appears that this understanding of the adoption of sportswear is relative to those in the fashionable 'know' and those who are not.

56

PLAY

58

59

60

PERFORMANCE
V
PERFORMATIVITY

61

62

One of the main similarities between fashion and sport is that they both strive for pleasure and play, albeit in very different ways. In sport, this is manifested through bodily performance, which supposedly carries an underlying value of purpose and is associated with a rational masculinity. In fashion, on the other hand, sartorial performativity – the performance of clothes – is often perceived as trivial and linked to a fickle femininity. By opposing these two notions visually in the form of a photo essay exploring the influence of eight different types of sport and adding examples of sportswear's manifestation in everyday street fashion, both the beginnings of an overlap and the uneasiness of the pairing become apparent.

Whilst the influence of sportswear on designer fashion is obvious, their ultimate compatibility is more uncertain. Vivienne Westwood's flamboyant interpretation of a hooded jacket paired with a take on eighteenth-century men's breeches in yellow admittedly has an interesting visual relationship with the eccentrically patterned outfits of jockeys, and Jean-Paul Gaultier's deconstructed tracksuit tops with a plunging back can be easily imagined on a young active urbanite. However, with the exception of these examples, and the work of designers such as Bernhard Willhelm and Jeremy Scott (whose entire design approach relies on the exaggeration of playfulness, sportswear being the perfect partner in crime to realize these ideas), high fashion's adaptations quite often seem forced.

The pictures of everyday street fashion, on the other hand, exemplify the possibilities of the performativity of sportswear in its

natural (or is it unnatural?) environment, and relate closely to Elizabeth Wilson's musings on the function of clothes:

Dress could play a part, for example, to either glue the false identity together on the surface, or to lend a theatrical and playacting aspect of the hallucinatory experience of the contemporary world; we become actors, inventing our costumes for each successive appearance, disguising the recalcitrant body we can never entirely transform.[1]

The way in which sportswear is worn when it is not on the sporting body is as a key accessory to the individuality of the consumer. Initially, because sportswear was comfortable and affordable, but increasingly it has acquired its own sartorial language.

The recurring theme of the performance of individuality within the relationship between fashion and sport is the impetus for the eight statements that follow the photo essay. Each contributor is or was closely involved in forging the ties between the two industries, whether as a designer, coolhunter, retailer, consumer or observer. These statements are of particular importance as they give an insight into this new casual sartorial language and highlight where the two industries really intersect: on the body of the fashionable consumer.

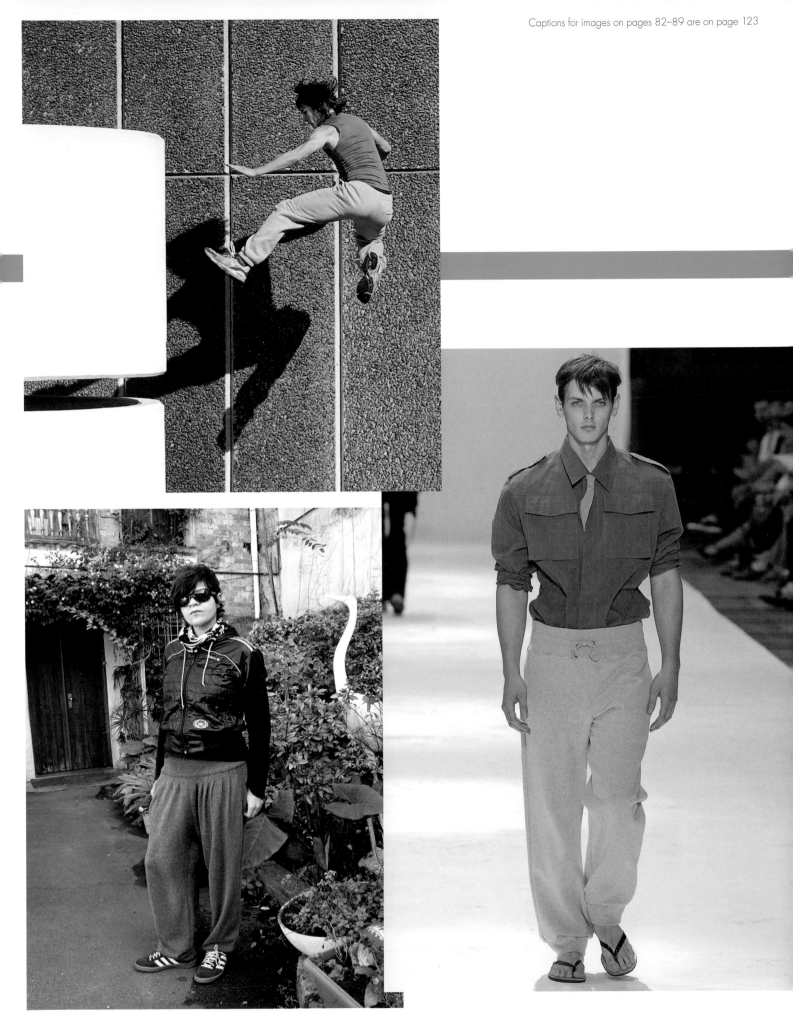

MIHARA YASUHIRO

Fashion Designer for Miharayasuhiro
and Collaborator with Puma

87

88

I think the relationship between fashion and sports has been intensifying recently. Whatever we wear, such as shoes and clothes, needs to be adapted to our environment: during the summer, for example, people are more inclined to wear clothes made from materials less likely to induce sweat, while during the winter people prefer warm clothes that ideally should not be too heavy. As the sports industry always searches for the new and develops innovative materials, these have been increasingly incorporated into fashion. Classic and organic materials are still popular, but consumers will soon demand the opportunities new materials offer.

That is why I also think that the relationship of fashion and sport is very important. The development of these new materials is crucial to the sports industry, but increasingly also for the fashion industry. However, in my opinion, I do not think many designers are realizing the potential of these innovations. Most are following the same trends and recycling old ideas. I have always been creating whatever I want and using innovations wherever possible. This is because as a designer, I am here to create attractive clothes and shoes that will influence people.

Nowadays even sports companies take fashion and the fashionable consumer very seriously. Research into consumer behaviour and patterns forms a sizeable part of new product development within the sports companies. When I design apparel wear for Miharayasuhiro, I have my consumer in mind. I believe that being physically comfortable is not as important as being mentally comfortable, even though, in my opinion, fashion should contain both these two design elements. What the consumer really wants is high quality and meaning.

I think the future relationship of fashion and sport is convivial. In fact PPR (the French company that owns the Gucci group) have taken over Puma. This can only mean that it will not be possible for sports companies to do only sports. However, I do not think fashion and sport will ever merge completely – obviously, we will never play tennis in high heeled shoes or climb Mount Everest wearing a beautiful dress. There will always be a need for specific performance sports clothes and the investment into their development. Therefore I think fashion and sport have already created and showed us the result of their relationship. Sportswear for performance gradually changed to sportswear performed in the city. I think this is the result of fashion and sport now.

It is commonplace these days for sports companies to produce new lines or products with fashion designers or other creative people. In fact this is the key way to sell products. But I want to ask them: 'Where is your emotion in your products? How long will you continue to sell merely an image and impression of the brand?' It is this apparent paradox that interests me when designing for Puma. However, the fact that Puma was the first sports brand eager to collaborate with a fashion designer means they are committed to finding new ways of mixing fashion and sports DNA.

CHRIS LEE

Founder and Managing Director of Microzine

There has always been a link between fashion and sport. In the 1800 and 1900s people wore so-called 'sports jackets' for outdoor pursuits such as hunting, shooting and fishing. Were these jackets designed specifically for sports or were they formal jackets customized to suit a particular activity? By definition of the term 'sports fashion', the two are joined at the hip. One influences the other; then that idea will move on to the next level, and so on. The two have had strong connections over the years, but in the late 1970s and early 1980s 'casual wear' appeared for the first time, particularly in the UK. During this period people started to wear combinations of Adidas, Puma, Fila and Sergio Tacchini with the likes of Norfolk tweed jackets, Church's shoes, FU's, Levi's, Peter Storm and Lyle & Scott. Even today at Microzine I still ask myself whether I should class Lyle & Scott as 'sportswear' or 'fashion'.

By the early 1990s, when the popularity of such brands as Timberland and Rockport had started to take hold and sell in volume, the major sports companies began to take notice of this shift. Very quickly the likes of Ellesse and Fila, amongst others, were taking tennis shoes and changing their colours to catch the eye of the same consumer. At the same time,

fashion companies such as Ralph Lauren, Donna Karan and Prada (slightly later), all longing for a slice of this new growth market, developed their own replies to the sports/fashion phenomenon with Polo Sport, DKNY Active and Prada Sport. They all influenced each other through the materials they used, design cues, technologies, patterns and colours, and contributed to the burgeoning market at that time.

The 1980s saw the sports-casual phenomenon emerge, and in the 1990s sports lifestyle fashion continued the developing consumption of sports fashion. Everything the brands did was new, innovative and exciting, as was the whole business. Brands and designers had the biggest influence on the product that was offered. Adi Dassler's ethos was to make people run faster, jump higher and beat records at any level, not to see how many navy and white tracksuits he could sell.

The success of the sports/fashion market and the expansion of multiple retailers have meant that on the whole these retailers can dictate the sportswear items being produced. During the 1990s, you could only buy what the predominantly financially led retailers were prepared to stock. Many a good buyer has become a 'historical merchandiser' to the detriment of the consumer, meaning that only what sold last season will be bought for the next season, which prevents real change in merchandise taking place. It is no surprise that the majority of those multiples look very tired with navy, white and black stock throughout, as well as the fact that they are constantly on sale.

The reason why a brand becomes great is because it consistently produces innovative product, whether it is influenced by design, colour, materials or construction, and customers associated that with the brand come to trust in it, building brand loyalty. The future is in the hands of the independent retailers – be they supplier or retailer – who are more willing and able to challenge the status quo and who have a more emotive and creative point of difference. There is once again a demand for product that tells a story. This has come about because trends seem to last so long (too long) these days, and because too many people are wearing the same thing, owing to a mass-market approach by the multiples. We need less of more, not more of less.

90

89

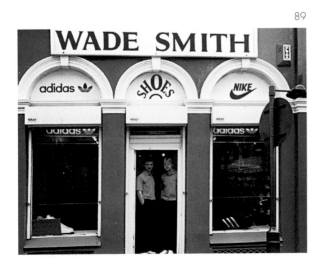

91   BEER. Fashion story for Japanese magazine
      Someonesgarden. Art direction and photography
      by Checkinit, 2007
92   A&P. Commission for AcceptandProceed. Art direction
      and photography by Checkinit, 2006

JENNY SCOTT

Consumer and Art Director at Checkinit

I was born in 1982, and since I was six I have been obsessed with the characters Ozone and Turbo in the movie *Breakdance*. I envied the whole Californian life-style – the weather, the music, the cars, the way Turbo wore his Converse baseball boots and Nike tracksuit pants with a conventional trench coat, and still looked so cool. This meant that, as well as wanting to be a dancer, I could not wait to be old enough to wear Lycra, high-tops and shell suits.

I never did become a dancer, but my early interest in sportswear grew with my love of music, specifically hip-hop and urban. With the need to be taken seriously within my role as Art Director, I now try and combine my love for street style with smarter key pieces. I do this by adding little accessories – having wild patterned acrylic nails tends to help. I take inspiration from everywhere, whether it is an antique market, a souvenir store or an MTV video. Thanks to the internet, music has become a lot more accessible, whether people are listening, producing or DJ-ing. This, in turn, creates subcultures and promotes musical crossover. Musicians are making things happen for themselves and are able to promote their work through tools such as

MySpace and their own band websites. No longer willing just to accept what is on offer, they are able to share their creativity and create and sell things for themselves and their peers without having to go through traditional channels. Hence, the corporate world is forced to pick up on and reproduce what these individuals have created, creating an endless choice of fashion and accessory combinations.

Sportswear is now as much about luxury as it is about comfort – although, admittedly, sport and exercise seem to take a back seat to fashionability. It is easy to put a pair of fresh new trainers on to dress down a glamorous top, giving the whole outfit an elegant and sexy street look. As new sports stars such as Lewis Hamilton introduce the lesser-known sport of Formula One to urban youth culture, new avenues for and influences on fashion will, I hope, inspire youngsters to take up more and different sporting activities, achieve higher goals and become more ambitious. The environment in which I work brings me into the realm of many fashionable people. The women that I am in daily contact with are body-conscious: gym activity is part of their lifestyle, and they are not willing to sacrifice style when going to the gym. So, it is lucky for them that designers are being seduced by major sportswear brands such as Adidas, Puma and Speedo. Alexander McQueen and Puma, Comme des Garçons and Speedo, and Marc Jacobs/Luella and Vans are just some of the most recent high-profile examples of fashion and sports-label collabo-rations. Adidas has been especially clever and, over the past few years, has built a strong and lasting link with Yohji Yamamoto on the Y-3 line, a collaboration that was taken seriously by the fashionistas and active types alike. Meanwhile, Stella McCartney's gymwear for Adidas gave the fashion designer new credibility in the sports arena. Sports and fashion collaborations can clearly work well for both sides.

Many so-called 'cool' fashion types may initially turn their noses up at these types of collaborations – until they see the results. I personally think when you put creative people from different fields together, it is very exciting to see what they spark off in each other. Just look at how Turbo and Ozone transformed rich daddy's girl Kelly Cupcake into ultimate ghetto female breakdancer.

91

92

93 NIKE 10AC. Styling by Koichiro Yamamoto.
    Photograph by WATARU
94 Caol Uno in UCS. Styling by Koichiro Yamamoto

CAOL UNO

MMA Fighter and designer of UCS

I became interested in fashion when I began wrestling in high-school club activities. I preferred wearing clothes such as Levi's, and at this time I also became conscious of the fashionability of tracksuits. Most people believe that this trend came about because of the influence of sports stars such as Michael Jordan, who inspired many young people to wear sports items with regular fashion.

When I became a professional fighter in October 1996, I became aware of the fact that many professional athletes were conscious of the attention their audiences paid to what they wore both during athletic performances and outside the arena. This is part of the reason why I started my own brand, UCS, as well as a collaboration with Nike called '10AC'. With both of these projects, I try to reflect my personal style, but also make what I cannot find in other brands. UCS better reflects what I would wear outside the ring – such as shirts, denims and caps – whereas the collaboration with Nike, 10AC, is more related to performance and training apparel.

The relationship between fashion and sport will evolve as each shares with the other its strongest elements. For example, sport will become more fashionably sophisticated whilst still retaining functionality. Fashion will become more innovatory and functional, whilst still remaining respectful of tradition and style.

93

94

It is my opinion that the relationship between fashion and sport has not intensified, but rather remained quite constant for a very long time. I am not sure when this relationship began. Fashion has always been drawing references and inspiration from sport, and even in technical sports apparel or footwear you can find a strong sense of fashion. I think this occurs because on a fundamental level, product is simply product. Only when fashion or sport are attached to something as a label do they sound dissimilar, but really there is little difference between the two. Both cater to a specific purpose or function, and are designed as such. The thought and development process for both is analytical in nature, and serves to better an individual design by means of refinement or detailing.

HIROKI NAKAMURA

Creative Director of Visvim

Customers have always wanted a stylish, functional, performance-based product regardless of what category or genre has been used to classify it. Maybe more recently fashion and sport marketing engines have been attempting to draw a distinction, but the reality is that if something works well and looks good, it does not really matter what you call it, it is the same thing. When a product is designed for a specific purpose, be it a dinner party, a summit party, a runway, etc., there is always a certain intention behind how that design will function. To me, because of this, there can never really be any borders in the design process. Only the labelling process differentiates the two…

95

96   Untitled. From *Back in the Days*.
       Photograph by Jamel Shabazz
97   Puma by Miharayasuhiro campaign, Autumn 2007.
       Photograph by Benjamin Alexander Huseby

The relationship between fashion and sport blossomed during an era of aspiration, when young people fixated with sport, music and fame perceived all of these as desirable escape routes from deteriorating inner-city lifestyles. Affiliating themselves with a sport or music scene, often by wearing a famous athlete's trademark apparel, or by mimicking a popular artist's style, young people would emulate their icons in the hope of earning kudos amongst their peers.

The linkage and convergence between fashion and sports began to intensify in the early to mid-1980s. In that period sportswear producers awoke to the fact that they would undoubtedly sell more if they catered to the true demand, the demand from the subcultures. At street level, personal style choices were driving the trend for adopting sportswear as key in a uniform of acceptability. At that point the passion for making money threatened to outgrow the passion for the previously purist sport performance product development. Side-stepping into a slipstream of business expansion, wealth creation and hyper-marketing, many sportswear brands adjusted the way that they would operate and the way in which they would consider their product.

Innovation in brand strategy and the growing influence of marketing have enabled traditional sports brands to maintain a certain momentum, to continue moving forward at speed. By balancing their feed to consumers so carefully, offering both innovative and technologically advanced products, but also by listening to and acting upon regular consumer insights, successful brands have empowered themselves with the tools to respond to consumer interests. Brands know how consumers like to obtain and receive certain products, who might influence their purchasing behaviour, and which colours they want to wear or might consider wearing. On the other hand, fashion companies borrowed from sportswear brands in order to fuel their developments in the area of sports-inspired lifestyle products. Fashion brands created supply for a market admiring of the form, function and comfort of sportswear apparel but demanding additional elevated status. From this status followed a sense of security derived from the attachment of a fashionable label to their adoption of sports style.

The future of sport fashion will be geared neither toward sport nor fashion, but instead toward the provision of apparel to facilitate the performance of lifestyles. Many will look at it in an apocalyptic way, suggesting that the combination of aesthetic and technological advances in sport/fashion will provide for the performance of survival. In the shorter term, lifestyles will continue to become more and more demanding and more dynamic. Dualities will drive the demand for diversity in the application of the apparel with which we choose to adorn ourselves. Give me 'the suit' – a phrase I choose to use loosely, referring merely to co-ordinated upper and lower body coverings – that I can run or cycle to work in, then comfortably go about 12 hours of tasks, before casually ending the day in social surroundings, all whilst being protected from the raging elements.

STYLESNIPER

Youth Trend Observer and Commentator

96

97

98   Steven Vogel in Idiom/Burton Jacket,
     2.5L Polka Dot, 2007
99   Detail of Idiom/Burton Jacket, 2006

STEVEN VOGEL

Global Special Project Manager for
Burton and Author of the book *Streetwear*

98

99

In terms of youth culture, I think some of the earliest
examples of sports apparel becoming directly translated
to the streets were in the 1970s, when basketball style,
especially its sneakers, became not only the choice outfit
but also a uniform. You need only think about Adidas
Superstars and Run DMC, a relationship best expressed
in their song 'My Adidas' and in the fact that they were the
first music band officially sponsored by Adidas (although
much later than the release of the song). Of course, there
were previous examples of athletic apparel worn as daily
fashion – Chuck Taylor's in the 1960s, for one – but the
impact basketball had was much broader and is still being
felt today. Skateboarding, and the look of a skateboarder,
another key casual influence, reached its height of
popularity in the early 1990s, when the X-Games propelled
skateboarding into the houses of every person with cable.
Nevertheless, in comparison to hip-hop and its 'look',
skateboarding has never had quite the same impact, even
though no one can deny that the baggy jeans, Vans and T-
shirt have been adopted worldwide.

In the case of the above examples, sports companies
definitely responded to what the customer wanted. Yet
for a long time, Nike and Adidas ignored the youth culture
demand. Considering the grass-roots popularity these two
brands enjoyed, it is quite amusing to think how long it took
them fully to engage youth culture through their marketing.
In fact, it took the better part of 20 years before the
companies caught on and catered, in terms of production
and marketing, to the kids out there buying their shoes. This
has drastically changed in the past eight years, however:
sports companies have smartened up and tried to identify
upcoming trends, and have geared their designs towards
those target groups.

I believe that the relationship between fashion and sport
will remain the same. Most sports apparel will not translate
into the mainstream fashion or apparel market. However,
clothing made for athletes – functional items – have been
an inspiration to fashion and youth cultures for a long time.
You can tell by looking at runway shows, and by how the
majority of high-end designers such as Prada incorporate
elements of functional clothing into their collections as an
example of this. In terms of the youth market, most of the
time functionality translates directly into young people's
lives, since they need the apparel to facilitate activities
such as skateboarding, snowboarding and BMX.

The majority of niche brands that cater to these sports
have caught on to this fact. In the past five years, some
have developed very fashionable technical outerwear
visible in such brands as Acronym and Idiom for Burton.
Brands like these are the future of this type of clothing; their
work appeals to fashionable people and snowboarders
alike, since both collections have the technical elements that
fulfil the requirements set forth by their environment without
looking like the typical outerwear brands of the past.

PASCAL
MONFORT

Consumer Culture Manager (Nike France) and Lecturer
in Fashion Sociology & History and Fashion & Music

Even if, since the 1980s, sports brands have occupied a privileged place in the hearts and wardrobes of teenagers, the relationship between fashion and sports intensified, in France, during the second half of the 1990s. During this decade, it became 'stylistically correct' to wear sneakers for every occasion. The 'cult' Adidas Gazelle was the first sneaker to become a consensual fashion accessory. It was first worn by trendy and creative adults, artists, people from communications careers and employers of start-up companies, who pushed it to become the symbol of a new kind of success, that of a new kind of yuppie: 'over-ambitious' yet 'cool'.

Shortly after, *Elle* magazine made a cover featuring the 'TOP Models' of the moment wearing the 'three stripes': it marked a big change. Even Inès de la Fressange, ex-model for Chanel, creator of and muse to French bourgeois elegance, announced that she hardly took them off. From this point, even the most conservative consumers made the audacious adventure of going to work in sneakers. All the fashion magazines tuned in, and the sport shoe became the accessory, the ultimate touch of glamour. At the opening of the shop Colette in 1997, a temple of fashion and luxury, the retailer's sneakers were the main subject of conversation among attendees. On the ground floor, the shoes: New Balance, Nike and Adidas ruled like kings. The same year, at Yohji Yamamoto, one wears the black suit with silver Nike Air Max (Y-3 does not exist yet) as a uniform. Meanwhile, at Comme des Garçons, the futuristic Reebok Fury is the unanimous statement. The 'influencers' set the tone and all France adopts the sneaker. Sport has become chic, and fits with fashion. This change is not only the result of the offer that sports brands propose. Numerous big commercial successes have been made on 'ancestral' products. Nowadays, while the prowess of technology and the virtuosi designs adorn the shop windows, the item that sells the most is the Converse, and it was designed about a hundred years ago. What has changed is the mentality of sports brands. They now have to compete alongside the fashion industry. They have to anticipate the cultural currents, understand the socio-styles and decipher the codes of the time in order to better serve the versatile and connoisseur consumer and lead the trends.

Sports and fashion have become an inseparable couple because the body is at the centre of the concerns of fashion. Luxury brands have understood it. Chanel, Prada, Dior, Hermès, Balenciaga, Louis Vuitton, Gucci and many others have launched their own sportswear collections, which have become an inescapable element of modernity. This market consequently represents a gigantic commercial opportunity that has not reached its apogee yet.

The future of the 'sport and fashion' coupling will be, like its time, as much spiritual and ethical as hyper-technological. All in all, this union seems, henceforth, eternal.

Translation by Chloé Salvago

NARCISSISM AND OBSESSION

102

This section serves as a conclusion to the previous explorations and its theme is purposely not set up as an opposition. Rather, the pairing of the two words 'Narcissism' and 'Obsession' is complementary, and points to the area of design and marketing where fashion and sportswear coexist most comfortably: the advertising and consumption of sports-inspired menswear menswear and sport-related products. Most modern male dress is derived from clothes designed for activity, from the abandonment of French court clothes for the more 'simple' English country clothes in the late eighteenth century to the more obvious adaptation of formal clothes to suit increasingly active lifestyles in the late nineteenth century.[1] Women's fashion, on the other hand, has a less direct relationship with sportswear. It has more gradually integrated aspects of design developed through sport innovation – as can be seen in the use of jersey and nylon fabrics by designers such as Coco Chanel and Claire McCardell, for example – but has rarely fully embraced the idea of leisurewear as high fashion. Whether or not this can be attributed to antiquated notions of femininity is not central to this exploration, but it does allow for a related question – why fashion and sport sit so closely and easily together within the design and advertising of fashionable products for men.

Both Oliver Winchester's exploration of 'The Pleasures of Spectatorship' and Mark Simpson's essay on what he terms 'Sporno' firmly steer our attention back towards the sporting body, and investigate the recent overt sexualization of sports personalities within advertising. Whilst Winchester's focus is the adoration of the athletic body, at its

Previous page
101   Thierry Henry for *Arena Homme Plus*.
      Photograph by Alasdair McLellan

102   Happy Victims. Nike. Photograph by Kyoichi Tsuzuki

most obvious in the context of the Olympics, and the changes now occurring in the way in which men look at men, Simpson takes this idea further. In his journalistic opinion piece he looks at examples of advertising campaigns, including those for Dolce & Gabbana underwear featuring Italian footballers in their dressing room, and the images of David James and David Beckham posing for Armani. His essay addresses the question of whether it is now acceptable for men to look at men because the hypermasculinity that sport offers legitimizes it socially, or whether it still remains an uncomfortable sight.

The safety net that sport provides certainly appears to have freed men from the former social constraints they faced when engaging with clothes. Somehow, it has encouraged male narcissism in a way that supersedes working out in the gym to obtain the perfect physique. Looking good, being individual without standing out too much, and an immaculate attention to detail as a matter of daily routine have always traditionally contributed to the successful styling of a young man, but contemporary sportswear has added an element of playfulness in terms of colour, cut and pattern which, until recently, was exclusive to women. Philosopher Gilles Lipovetsky's thoughts on menswear emphasize this:

But the real novelty lies chiefly in the extra-ordinary development of sportswear. With mass leisure apparel, men's clothing has made its authentic entrance into the cycle of fashion, marked by frequent changes, compulsory originality, and playfulness.[2]

The abundance of choice within the arena of sports apparel, and the obsessions to which this gives rise, are highlighted through Takeharu Sato's focus on the Japanese brand F.C.R.B., which stands for Football Club Real Bristol. The idea for this brand was born out of fashion designer Hirofumi Kiyonaga's two passions: football, and the music culture of the city of Bristol. Sato's piece unpicks the working of this unusual brand, for whose protagonists – the football team – the designer has created various virtual incarnations. It also illuminates the final aspect of this book and exhibition, which looks at how the enormous selection of apparel on offer and the power of branding also facilitate the obsessive collecting of sportwear goods, whether these are of a particular brand (as the image of an excessive Nike consumer shows) or, just simply, trainers. The status of the one-off, limited edition or cult design sneaker within the relationship of fashion and sport is crucial, since it indicates the point at which sportswear's function has become almost redundant. Hence, a short interview and the portrait of sneaker collector Kish Patel in the midst of a small part of his expansive collection of trainers forms the somehow poignant conclusion to this publication.

THE PLEASURES OF SPECTATORSHIP

OLIVER WINCHESTER

105

Feminist film theory tells us that straight men look and that women are looked at. A man's gaze is always active; it disinterestedly objectifies women as passive objects for visual consumption. Consequently, so the story goes, men do not look at each other, do not consume each other's bodies – unless they are 'queer', that is. However, sports spectatorship has traditionally stood as the single socially acceptable opportunity for men to look at each other's bodies safe from accusations of homosexuality. The act of gazing at the invariably supple, defined and youthful male sporting body has achieved this peculiar immunity thanks to the athletic body's loaded meaning within society.

Functioning as a highly symbolic visual shorthand for various socially constructed notions of discipline, health and productivity, the sporting body is asexual, pure, almost god-like in its embodiment of higher Platonic ideals of beauty. Time and effort are expended in the quest for sporting success, personal improvement and an affirmation of self-worth through hard work. It is the dynamism of these exertions, written upon the body's surface, that enables men to consume such images without censure. As art historian Paul Jobling has noted, 'images of men must disavow… passivity if they are to be kept in line with dominant ideas of masculinity-as-activity.'[1] Moreover 'the fetish of admiring body parts ("look at those triceps") gives [men] a scientistic pleasure and alibi'.[2] Men are able to watch semi-naked bodies swim, run, box and dive, safe in a collective understanding of the deeper significance of these activities. The pleasures of sports

106 Olympic pole vaulter Tom Hintinauss posing
for Calvin Klein campaign, 1983. Photograph
by Bruce Weber
107 Ralph Lauren Polo campaign, 1991.
Photograph by Bruce Weber

107

spectatorship clearly stem from more than the mere act of looking.

This superior level of meaning attributed to sports and the body is perhaps most clearly expressed in the Olympic movement. The first modern-day Olympic Games, held in Athens in 1896 and comprising 14 competing nations, was envisaged by its founder, Pierre de Coubertin, as an egalitarian, chivalrous and politically significant event. Participating in the gentlemanly act of sporting contest, until 1904 the winner was awarded a silver medal and laurel crown, a gesture that explicitly referenced the ancient games and the universality of the sports competition as a Platonic form. Moreover, the Olympic Creed reads 'the most important thing in the Olympic Games is not to win but to take part, just as the most important thing in life is not the triumph but the struggle. The essential thing is not to have conquered but to have fought well'.[3] Sports and ethics thus combine to form a powerful justification for men to look at men.

Yet this theatrical and highly principled alibi for the male gaze no longer seems so secure. Increasingly since the 1980s fashion photography has revelled in male sexual ambiguities and overt homoeroticism, and languorous images of sporting celebrity endorsements are commonplace. Bruce Weber's highly eroticized photograph of the Olympic pole vaulter Tom Hintinauss, produced for a Calvin Klein advert of 1983, clearly shows the body's move from an active and purposeful subject to a sexually potent passive object. Images such as these seek to exploit potential sexual ambiguities rather than resolve them.

The machismo of spectatorship is called into question as sportsmen undress and offer up their bodies as fashion mannequins. Such men are increasingly aware of themselves as objects of desire, and advertising has adapted to seduce heterosexual consumers with appropriately narcissistic images. A slippage has occurred within the male gaze.

This shift is derived in part from changing attitudes towards the body, health and fitness. Thanks to the growth of the fitness industry and gym membership, men's relationship to their bodies has altered. The body no longer serves as a symbolic repository of collectively held abstract principles but as an insular and egotistical image of self-definition through consumption: the body co-opted by the lifestyle industry presents a further opportunity for authentic self-expression. As sociologist Roberta Sassatelli has commented, 'the body is seen as an instrument to be used rather than a source of value to be preserved, and is worked on at the level of forces rather than at the level of signs'.[4] Spectatorship takes on the character of consumer choice, with its empty disinterestedness. With the commodification of the beautiful sporting body and the withering of their collective ethical alibi, straight men looking at other men might now, more than ever, feel envious… and maybe a little turned on?

SPORNO

MARK SIMPSON

You might think that it was Italy's greater ball skills, or stamina, or team spirit, that won them the last World Cup. But you would be wrong. Clearly, explicitly, thrillingly, what won it for the Italians was not so much their sporting spirit as their *sporno spirit*. In the run-up to the tournament, some especially fit players from the Italian team took time off from their training and did something much more useful: they recruited Dolce & Gabbana (or was it the other way around?) to produce a spornographic fashion shoot of them all oiled up and ready for us. In hindsight, we can see that the world was already grovelling at their feet from that moment on.

Sporno, the post-metrosexual aesthetic that sports and advertising are using to sell us the male body is, well, *irresistible*. Even for the French – who were, let's face it, a much plainer bunch. First Portugal devastate England because Ronaldo is better looking than Becks and far swoonier than Rooney, then Italy trounce France because the punters would much rather celebrate with the sweaty Italian stallions in the locker-room. The best men definitely won.

In a spornographic age it's no longer enough for the male body to be presented to us by consumerism as merely desirable, or desiring to be desired, as it was in the early days of nakedly narcissistic male metrosexuality. This masculine coquettish-ness, pleasing as it is, no longer offers an intense enough image. Or provokes enough lust. It's just not very shocking or arousing any more. In fact, it's just too… *normal*. To get our attention these days the sporting male body has to promise us nothing less than an immaculately groomed, waxed and pumped group session in the showers. But of course, because this is sporno and not actual pornography, it remains just that: a promise. Advertising and fashion are less interested in making a fetish of the potent male body than its *underwear*: commodity fetishism is usually the name of the sporno game.

However, the homoprovocative nature of sporno is much less easy to disavow than it was in metrosexuality, which could pretend when it wanted to that it was 'straight' and something entirely for the ladies. Where metrosexual imagery stole slyly from soft gay porn, sporno blatantly references hard gay porn.

Actually, you might be forgiven for thinking sport *is* the new gay porn. Sportsmen are now openly acknowledging and flirting with their gay fans, à la David Beckham and fellow footballer and coquettish Calvin Klein underwear model Freddie Ljungberg. Both of these officially heterosexual thoroughbreds have posed for spreads in gay magazines (Ljungberg appeared on the cover of *Attitude* in April 2006, Beckham in 2002), albeit sporting more clothes than they usually wear when appearing on the side of buses. Beefy England Rugby ace and married father of two Ben Cohen has explicitly marketed a calendar of sexy pics of himself at gay men, and talks of 'embracing his gay fans'.[1] Some, like Becks and smoothly-muscled Welsh Rugby ace Gavin Henson have even apparently argued over them.[2]

Being found desirable by gay men, once a source of ridicule and anger, now seems to mean you are worthy

not just of love but also of large amounts of cash. A whole new generation of young bucks, from twinky soccer players such as Manchester United's Cristiano Ronaldo, who has modelled for Pepe, and Chelsea's Fabulous Frankie 'Legs' Lampard, to rougher prospects such as Joe Cole and A.C. Milan's Kakà posing for Samsung and Armani jeans respectively, and the naked, pneumatic rugby 'pros' of the legendary *Dieux du Stade* calendars, seems to be actively pursuing Beckham's and Ljungberg's male sex-object, slightly tarty, status.

Being equal opportunity flirts, today's sporno stars want to turn *everyone* on. Partly because sportsmen, like porn stars, are by definition show-offs, but more particularly because it means more money, more power, more endorsements, more kudos. Sporno exploits the corporate showbiz direction that sport is moving in, as well as the undifferentiated nature of desire in a media-saturated, mirrored-ceiling world – and inflates their career portfolio to gargantuan proportions. Why is Euro soccer star Beckham a household name in the United States, a country that generally has less interest in soccer than socialism? Why did his recent move to the US to play for a team most Americans had never hear of provoke so much breathless coverage in the US media? Some may argue that is was not down to his soccer skills, but rather his *sporno* skills. Pictures of him semi-naked in *Vanity Fair*, or in *W* magazine, sporting skin-tight trousers that nevertheless seem to be somehow pulling themselves off, or that naked campaign for Motorola, in which the mobile phone dangles tantalizingly

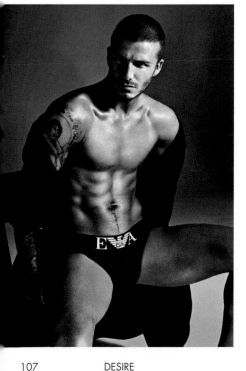

109

110

between his pert nipples, seem to be more ubiquitous, not to mention more stirring, than images of him playing football.

And what could be more American? Sporno stars are pushy young hustlers who are happy to be ogled undressed on Times Square billboards or in *Vanity Fair* – advertising a willingness to put out, or at least get it out, to get ahead. In campaigns like Ljungberg's Calvin Klein unforgettable underwear posters of 2006 or Beckham's globally gawked Armani briefs ads of 2008, their bodies and their bulges, blown up to gigantic proportions, are rammed down our throats by advertising. Most of us don't appear to be gagging, however. And if we did find any of this hard to swallow, we could always reach for a nice cool, creamy Becks – recently hired as the (topless) face of the US's long-running 'Got Milk?' campaign.

The male body has been well and truly, not to mention tastily, commodified. After decades of being fetishized by gay men, jocks are now fetishizing themselves. It was probably inevitable. Men are traditionally the more visual of the sexes – and by far the greatest consumers of porn. So why not cut out the middle-women and pornolize yourself?

Because of the fantastical masculine potency of sporno, millions of boys and men around the world are excitedly buying clothes and underwear because they are worn or endorsed by their hero. In a consumerist, mediated world where envy and desire become deliberately, profitably blurred, the once crucial distinction of whether they *want* him or want to *be* him it makes no

commercial difference — so long as they buy and wear his briefs. And how could a guy, any guy, *not* have their head turned by a sporno star? Sporno stars have everything a man could want today: youth, vigour, money, fame, looks, equally beautiful bosom buddies and the numbers for top photographers and stylists.

The people who essentially invented sport, the Ancient Greeks, certainly thought the male athlete the greatest head-turner. For them, sport was an opportunity to worship and admire the beauty of the youthful male form, which in turn represented the freedom of the human spirit. They thought it natural that men would find the youthful athletic male form inspiring and desirable, and an essential part of the pleasure of sport. Most sports competitions, including the original Olympics, were conducted naked: clothes spoiled the experience, for athlete *and* spectator. Much of their muscular art was a classical antecedent of today's sporno.

Admittedly though, many Greeks would probably have been scandalized by the keenness of today's golden young athletes to pose for images designed to inflame lust — and cash purchases. Plato for one would certainly have been aghast at the neo-classical shamelessness of *Dieux du Stade* ('Gods of the Stadium'). The phenomenally successful, luxurious calendars feature the Paris-based Stade Français rugby team and various well-endowed sporting guest stars from around the world re-enacting, you may be thinking, the plot of every sports-themed gay porn vid, photographed by fashion photographers such as Mariano Vivanco, responsible for the particularly striking 2007 images. If these inflammatory

calendars weren't in tasteful black-and-white, they'd have to be sold in adult bookstores. Shot in musty locker rooms, the stark-naked 'gods' clutch strategically placed, not to mention bragging, rugby balls and gaze longingly into the camera or into each other's eyes.

Such brazen behaviour has only enhanced the careers of these rugger buggers. Frédérik Michalak and his hypnotically tattooed butt's starring role in an early DVD showing the making of the *Dieux du Stade* calendar, has helped land him modelling contracts for Christian Lacroix, a French condom line endorsement deal, as well as becoming the expensive face of Biotherm Homme and the sporting package for a skimpy underwear line.

No doubt the Greeks would have been shocked even more by the way that women are openly enjoying these homoprovocative images too. In fact, the *Dieux du Stade* calendars were originally part of a marketing plan to update and widen the appeal of French rugby, particularly for women, and have proved massively popular: the 2007 calendar reportedly sold 200,000 copies. But the sporno-graphic eye of *Dieux du Stade* is quite deliberately, quite flagrantly un-straight. Partly because some of today's women are being turned on to the voyeuristic charms of male-on-male action (in an echo perhaps of their boyfriends' interest in female-on-female action), partly because it gets attention — 'whatarethoseguysdoing!', and partly because, as we've seen, the adoration of gay men is the key to the successful marketing of the male body. But mostly because this all-male exhibitionism, whomever it's directed toward, gay/ straight/bi/female/male/mineral, is so charmingly, submissively keen to please – especially from guys who live through action and the urge to dominate.

Check out the *Dieux du Stade: Making Of the 2004 Calendar* DVD, or the *Making of* DVD from any year really, and see them obediently adopting the gay porno poses requested of them by the photographer, head placed on buddy's shoulders, or head at buddy's waist, hands on his perfectly formed buttocks. The uninhibitedness of the rugby players, in part a function of the physical intimacy of the game itself, ends up being deliciously suited to the visual uninhibitedness of our times. How things – or rather, thighs – have changed. In the United Kingdom rugby traditionally was the sport of hairy beer monsters with nowhere else to go on a Saturday. But with professionalization, players, particularly backs, have become younger, fitter, and self-consciously sexier and their dance-cards are as full as their biceps. Blond, buffed, green-eyed England International player Josh Lewsey, sporting a jaw so square you could use it to point walls and an arse so proud you could stand your pint on, has been deployed to interest rugby fans in bulging lycra. A giant, god-like blow-up 'bronze' statue of him was erected outside Twickenham rugby stadium in 2006 by his sponsor Nike. Rugby fans queuing for their tickets had the distracting pleasure of gazing up between Josh's towering, flared thighs and at his divine abs and pecs, naughtily outlined by a skin-tight top.

The England rugby strip has also apparently been given a *Queer Eye* makeover.

Banished forever are their baggy, shapeless beer-towel rugby shirts, (see the one modelled by Ben Cohen in 2000), replaced by a form-hugging strip that might well have been designed by Jean Paul Gaultier. Understandably, England's new sporno kit dazzled the opposition: in 2003, the year the team debuted it, England won the Rugby World Cup for the first time ever. The latest version of it, introduced for the 2007 World Cup, saw them achieve second place despite being written off beforehand by pundits. No doubt this astonishing turnaround was down to their new strip being being even tighter than before and including a saucy red arrow/ swoosh from armpit to the edge of the opposite thigh, reportedly designed to confuse opposing players. Too right – they won't know whether to tackle them or kiss them. A confusion that seemed to be exploited, albeit unwittingly, by the 'C'est so Paris' humorous advertising campaign promoting the 2007 World Cup, which featured snogging rugby players and the jokey tagline 'Paris: City of Love' (ironically, the only unlikely and unconvincing aspect of the campaign was the unattractiveness of the fake rugby players compared to the 'real' *Dieux du Stade* thing).

In the more moneyed world of football, which has been a much bigger business for much longer, the eye-catching potency of a sporno star seems to have disorientated even the tough no-nonsense guys who manage football clubs – until you look at the bottom line. Despite somewhat inconsistent performances on the pitch, David Beckham is the world's most highly paid soccer player and the best known – because of his off-pitch pouting (most recently confirmed by his 2007 £20 million Armani underwear

114

113

115

deal). His purchase in 2003 by Spain's Real Madrid made them the most profitable soccer club in the world (replacing Manchester United – Beckham's previous club). Beckham is an object of global desire, and his merchandise moves even faster than his hips. After making (reportedly) the biggest sports deal in history at £128 million, American team LA Galaxy is his new sporno studio, and he their Number One box cover star.

There is, however, another way in which British soccer players are finding themselves and their athletic prowess paraded on the front pages. A slew of kiss-and-tell articles have appeared in the tabloids in recent years about the penchant our young sportsmen have for sharing a young female groupie with several other team mates. Simultaneously. Often videoing the proceedings. Sporting gods in naked, adult video action with other sporting gods. No wonder the tabs and the public got so excited. In recreating the more than slightly homoerotic straight 'gang-bang' porn that they, like many other young men today are downloading from the Net, footballers are, wittingly or not, realizing the fantasy underpinning sporno itself.

Things reached their logical, if slightly *Footballers Wives* conclusion – their spornographic money shot – in 2006 when lurid stories were 'splashed' across the tabloids about a 'secretly shot film' allegedly showing several globally famous (but unnamed) English soccer stars engaging in a 'gay sex orgy', in which expensive limited edition mobile phones were supposedly used as 'sex toys'.[3] Regardless of the fact or feverish fantasy of this story, no one seemed to be able to get enough of it. Except perhaps the footballers themselves – who were not only not making any money out of this particular sporno spin-off, but also faced the threat of losing earning potential as a result of the scandal (British libel laws however quickly came to the rescue providing at least one player with a large, undisclosed sum).[4] The response of many fans on the terrace in the form of vicious anti-gay taunts and the continued absence of any openly gay professional footballers, suggest that casual homophobia is as rampant in the culture as sporno itself – which is more than slightly ironic.

A generation of men may be entranced by images of glamorous, sporting males who so clearly, achingly, desire to be desired by all and sundry, but it seems the explicitly homoerotic implications of that still give quite a few of them the willies, especially in the highly strung world of football.

Sporno stars themselves, moving in their celebrity circles, probably don't care two hoots whether a fellow player prefers bedroom partners with the same-shaped tackle, and may even be as pansexual as their advertising and fashion tastes portrays them, but they worry very much about what their fans will think. After all, this is show business, darling, and you can't afford to alienate your audience – or, paradoxically, those homoerotic spornographic endorsement deals. While the statements of gay-friendly soccer stars such as Beckham and Ljungberg (and Cohen and Henson in rugby) have been sincere and helpful, thus far, actual homosex, or even bisex, rather than the *faux* variety proffered by advertising appears to still be beyond

the pale. Sporno stars may pose gay but until now all of them have had to be officially totally heterosexual – as do all pro footballers.

Perhaps this is also the reason today's soccer stars, who appear, way 'gayer' than their predecessors – according to *The Sun*, Manchester United's locker rooms have recently had to be modified to make room for players' 'manbags', because, apparently, 'they use more cosmetics than their wives'[5] – no longer kiss one another passionately after a goal is scored like they did just a few years ago. They have to maintain the impression, like many actual porn stars, that they're only gay for pay.

As for the paymasters themselves, the fashion brands, while they certainly wish to encourage a change in masculine attitudes towards fashion, the male body and erotics, it could be argued that a certain amount of homophobia works to their benefit here: both making sporno advertising images more arresting, and also helping to displace any homoerotic feelings/anxiety they provoke safely into commodity fetishism: buying the product instead of the lifestyle. 'Of course I don't want the athlete's looks/face/body/packet', the hetero male viewer/voyeur of sporno perhaps says to themselves – 'I want his pants'.

Nevertheless, these are interesting if somewhat conflicted times. We shouldn't underestimate how far we've come and how dramatically attitudes in traditional male past-times such as football and rugby have changed in the last decade as a result of their collision with the world of fashion, celebrity and consumerism.

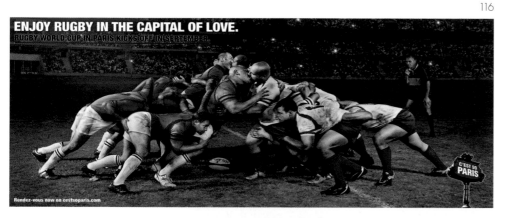

116

117

118

Sporting male heroes have enthusiastically taken up shockingly exhibitionistic sex-object poses in the global media that once were anathema for most men because they were seen as 'girly', 'slutty' or 'homo'. Or, what was much the same emasculating taboo in the male mind: *passive*.

This still is a taboo, for some. As one outraged middle-aged male BBC sports presenter thundered recently in *The Sun* about Beck's Armani ad: 'You've got money, status, respect and fame – then someone says: "Armani want you to do a picture wearing tight white pants with your legs as wide open as the hole in England's defence." Why would you say yes?'[6]

Actually, in a spornographic age, the question should rather be: *why on earth would you say no?*

119 Hirofumi Kiyonaga, designer of F.C.R.B.
and SOPHNET. Photograph by Yasuyuki Takaki
120 F.C.R.B. 'Team Photo', Autumn/Winter 2001–2.
Photograph by P.M. Ken
121 F.C.R.B. 'at Bristol Station', Autumn/Winter 2002–3.
Photograph by P.M. Ken

119

120

F.C.R.B.
OBSESSIVE
IMAGINATION

TAKEHARU
SATO

The collaboration between Nike and F.C.R.B. was born out of fashion designer Hirofumi Kiyonaga's two obsessions: football, and music culture in Bristol. F.C.R.B., which stands for Football Club Real Bristol and is the sub-line to his main design venture SOPHNET., represents the only longstanding relationship the global company Nike has had with a fashion company (it launched in 2000), and it remains unique, as all products bear both the Nike and the F.C.R.B. logo. The brand focuses exclusively on the Japanese market, a possible reason for the success of this collaboration, as it means that the identity of the global brand Nike is not necessarily compromised.

The obsessive nature of this project is manifested in the various ways in which the F.C.R.B. team is brought to life. Even though his company sponsors the real football team Oita Trinita, which is based in Kiyonaga's home town, he created another, semi-virtual football team for the brand. It consists of small plastic figurines, photographed by fashion photographer P.M. Ken and then digitally dressed in the clothes of the season and manipulated into a setting. The team is featured in each season's catalogue in various locations, such as 'Bristol town centre', 'Bristol train station', their 'stadium' and 'on tour' at Munich's Allianz Arena.

Kiyonaga also initiated a virtual stadium for the F.C.R.B. team with architect Nobuo Araki (who also designs all SOPHNET. shops). Entitled 'F.C.R.B. Stadium Project', it was exhibited in the National Museum of Emerging Science and Innovation in Tokyo in 2004.

121

FASHION V SPORT

122   F.C.R.B. Stadium Project in collaboration
       with architect Nobuo Araki, exhibited at
       the National Museum of Emerging Science
       and Innovation in 2004. Photograph by
       Yasuhide Kuge
123–124 Kojiro Hyuga as captain of F.C.R.B. and
       Captain Tsubasa wearing SOPHNET.
       Cover of Spring/Summer 2007 catalogue.
       Created by manga artist Yoichi Takahashi

The brand first produced the stadium goods to sell so that part of the proceeds could be invested in the future real construction of the stadium.

As a result anyone who bought the products genuinely became a participant in the realization of the ideal football club and stadium.

The concept of the stadium is described by Nobuo Araki in its press release:

The Silent Stadium – the fundamental concept of its stadium construction is a 'digging in the ground and mounting the dug out earth and sand around the hole. When the stadium is not in use anymore the mounted earth and sand will be brought back where they were and the stadium itself will resolve into its elements and the natural landscape will return.'

The construction process with architectural temporality is the result of relation to the self-healing ability of the earth. The environmental awareness displayed by this project is also evident in the fact that the American fabric company DuPont was involved in the collaboration. This resulted in the incorporation of a material called Biomax®, which is made of biodegradable plastic.

Out of Kiyonaga's obsession with football emerged another creative twist to this project, in the form of a further collaboration with Yoichi Takahashi, the manga cartoon artist. Takahashi is most famous for his story about Tsubasa, a football-obsessed Japanese boy, who becomes Captain

124

123

Tsubasa, captain of the Japanese national football team. For this exhibition he created an original manga comic actualizing a match between Tsubasa's team and F.C.R.B., which features Tsubasa's rival Kojiro Hyuga as captain of F.C.R.B. On the poster and on the front of that season's catalogue, the character Tsubasa wears SOPHNET. and Hyuga wears F.C.R.B.

The computer football game 'Winning 11' (or 'Pro-evolution soccer', as it is more widely known) provoked quite a few questions in the international gaming community when, in its fifth edition, an unknown team called F.C.R.B. appeared amongst the likes of Arsenal and Manchester United. This further example of Kiyonaga's passion for his ideal team even exceeds fellow fashion designer Dirk Bikkembergs's obsession with football, which was made most apparent in the purchase of and subsequent kit design for Italian football team F.C. Fossombrone. Hirofumi Kiyonaga's obsession with football has not only driven a unique fashion and sport brand collaboration, but also a project that embodies the dreams of so many young men today.

126

Opposite
127 Kish Patel, trainer collector. Styling by Tony
Charalambous. Photograph by Patricia Niven

KISH PATEL: TRAINER COLLECTOR

Interviewed by Ligaya Salazar

LS How long have you been collecting trainers?
KP The first pair of kicks I bought was around 1982, but I really got into the whole scene around 1988. Also when I was skating, I would go through trainers rapidly, which may have kick-started my impulse to buy more than the average consumer.

LS What sparked your interest in trainers?
KP It was a combination of my interest in hip hop and football. Both cultures have a deep-rooted affinity with trainers… from wearing them for breakin', or on the terraces, or for a kick about in the park. No one at the time could envisage that trainers would be collectable and also desired outside of these scenes.

LS How many pairs of trainers do you own?
KP Over 1000; I'm not sure of the exact figure as I've never taken the time to count every single pair.

LS What drives your continued interest in collecting?
KP I just love the various aesthetics of trainers and also the way they can complement different looks. The comfort factor is an issue. As well as the desire to own what I couldn't as a kid.

LS With the continuing changes in the sports footwear market, what do you think is the future of trainer-collecting?
KP I can see brands going into their heritage a lot more and reissuing even more models, but with new twists as well as their original look, and also applying old aesthetics to new concepts. The fascination with trainers will continue to grow and we are likely to see even more people adopting them as a part of their attire.

NOTES

Introduction
1   Wilson (1985), p.166
2   Martin (1998), p.13
3   Craik (2005), p.141
4   Skoggard (1998), p.59
5   Bedell (2003)
6   Cited in Bedell
7   He derives this from David
    Harvey's notion of 'flexible
    accumulation' developed
    in his influential book, *The
    Condition of Postmodernity*,
    published in 1990.
8   Skoggard, p.59
9   http://press.adidas.com/
    DesktopDefault.aspx/
    tabid-70/96_read919/
    (July 2004)
10 Wilson, p.154
11 Ibid., p.137
12 Gilbert (2000), p.8
13 Gladwell (1997)

Pure Gesture
1   Barthes (1993), p.25
2   Ibid., p.15
3   Hargreaves (1986), p.14
4   Ibid., pp.10–14. See also
    Horne (2006), p.4.
5   Lowerson (1993), p.2
6   Ibid.
7   Horne, pp.27–8
8   Breward (2003)
9   Campbell Warner (2006), p.3
10 Shannon (2006), pp.183–4
11 Johnston (2005), p.162.
    See also Anderson (2005),
    pp.283–303.
12 Bolton (2002), p.14
13 Craik (2005), p.145
14 Cunnington and Mansfield
    (1969), p.18
15 Ibid., p.50
16 Ibid., p.57
17 Lehmann (2000), p.xviii
18 Segal (1998), pp.173–218
19 Pavitt (2000), pp.156–75
20 Stern (2004), pp.53–4
21 Breward (2003), pp.67–70
22 Stern, pp.52–3
23 Ibid., p.54
24 Poirier (2003)
25 Tinling (1983), p.193
26 http://www.fredperry.com
27 http://www.lacoste.fr

28 Blake (1996), p.186
29 Ibid., p.145
30 Ricca (1983)
31 Ibid.
32 Campbell Warner, pp.104–37
33 Ibid., pp.46–9
34 Horwood (2002), pp.45–60
35 Campbell Warner, p.83
36 Martin and Khoda (1990),
    pp.28–36
37 Wilk (2006), p.258
38 Ibid., p.267
39 Craik, pp.166–8; Quinn
    (2002), pp.185–200
40 Breward (2004), pp.46–7
41 Smart (2005), p.3
42 Rojek (2001)
43 Smart, p.15
44 Hewitt and Baxter (2006),
    pp.43–58
45 Smart, p.17
46 Holt and Mason (2000),
    pp.176–7

*The author is very grateful for the
support of Ligaya Salazar and Oliver
Winchester in the research and editing
of this chapter.*

DARE
Tradition V Innovation
1   Craik (2005), p.139
2   Cited on BBC Sport (2004)
3   Speedo Press Release, Speedo
    launches world's fastest suit
    (March 9, 2004)

DISPLAY
Uniformity V Individuality
1   Scoper (2001), p.27
2   Lipovetsky (1994), p.123
3   Ibid., p.109

Standing out as one of the crowd
1   Woodward (2004), p.33
2   Simmel (1957), p.549
3   The interviews used in this essay
    are drawn from Murphy (2006).
4   Craik (2005), p.144
5   Craik, p.17
6   Warwick and Cavallero (1998),
    p.76; Wilson (1985)
7   Craik, p.144
8   Simmel (1971), p.271
9   Woodward (2005)

10 Veblen (1964), p.67
11 Lipovetsky, p.131
12 Woodward (2007)
13 Carter (2003)
14 Simmel (1957), p.549

PLAY
Performance V Performativity
1   Wilson (1992), p.8

DESIRE
Narcissism and Obsession
1   Laver (1995), pp.149, 202
2   Lipovetsky, p.107

The Pleasures of Spectatorship
1   Jobling, (2005), p.15
2   Miller (2006), p.413
3   http://www.olympic.org/uk/
    organisation/missions/
    charter_uk.asp
4   Sassatelli (2006), p.259

Sporno
1   http://www.outsports.com/
    people/2007/bencohen
    1106.htm
2   Baker (2005)
3   cited in Muir (2006)
4   Ibid.
5   http://www.thesun.co.uk/
    sol/homepage/news/article
    250650.ece
6   http://www.thesun.co.uk/
    sol/homepage/news/article
    568062.ece

IMAGE CREDITS

PLAY Photoessay, pages 82–9.
Images read top to bottom, left
to right:

Page 82

63 'Variitaions on Sport', *Vogue Italia*, April 2005. Photograph by Steve Hiett
64 Breakdancer in a cycling top at the UK Fresh Hip Hop event, London 1986. Photograph by Paul Hartnett
65 Spain's David Canada rides in front of Germany's Matthias Kessel, Tour de France, 16 July 2006. Photograph by Pascal Guyot

Page 83

66 Two young skinheads in front of a bench wearing Fred Perry shirts, c.1979. Photograph by John G. Byrne
67 Serena Williams, US Open, 7 September 2004. Photograph by Clive Brunskill
68 Lacoste, Spring/Summer 2004

Page 84

69 Y-3, Spring/Summer 2004
70 Steven Gerrard and Jihai Sun, Manchester City versus Liverpool, 14 April 2007. Photograph by Clive Brunskill
71 Young man wearing a Sweden football shirt, London 2007. Photograph by STYLESNIPER

Page 85

72 Vladimir Radmanovic and Udonis Haslem, Miami Heat versus Los Angeles Lakers, 15 January 2007. Photograph by Stephen Dunn
73 Young man in a London subway wearing a basketball vest. Photograph by STYLESNIPER
74 John Richmond, Spring/Summer 2007

Page 86

75 Couple on a Tokyo street, 2007. Photograph by Jennifer Pierce
76 EleyKishimoto for Ellesse, Autumn/Winter 2005–6
77 Liu Jiayu at the Sixth Asian Winter Games, 29 January 2007. Photograph by Adam Pretty

Page 87

78 Andy Macdonald, X Games Eleven, 5 August 2005. Photograph by Nick Laham
79 Skaters2, two boys with skateboards. Photograph by Vanessa Oguchi
80 Paul & Joe, Autumn/Winter 2007

Page 88

81 A breakdancer wearing red-and-white striped legwarmers, white shorts and a red vest at Funktup, December 2004. Photograph by Suzy Del Campo
82 Christian Dior, Couture, Autumn 2003
83 Bailarinas, Mexico City, 2007. Photograph by Itzel Valle: Zamuraika

Page 89

84 Parkour jumper at Hayward Gallery, London 2007. Photograph Jon Cartwright
85 Young woman in grey tracksuit bottoms and black jacket, Sao Paulo, 2006. Photograph by Amarilio Jr.
86 Dries van Noten, Spring/Summer 2007

© AllSport/Getty images: 104
© A World Beneath: 5
© Brett Booth: 53, 54, 55, 56, 71, 73
© Checkinit: 91, 92
© Christopher Moore/Catwalking. com: 27, 28, 29, 31, 35, 36, 37, 39, 41, 59, 60, 61, 62, 68, 69, 74, 76, 80, 82, 86
Courtesy of Adidas: 4, 6
Courtesy of BDDP & Fils agency: 116
Courtesy of CUBISM Inc.: 24, 25, 95
Courtesy of DRx: 43
Courtesy of Fashion News, Japan: 40
Courtesy of Fred Perry: 14
Courtesy of Giorgio Armani: 109, 110
Courtesy of Gyro Press: 44
Courtesy of Kim Jones: 26, 30, 32, 33
Courtesy of I-Saw: 42
Courtesy of Little Bear Inc.: 106, 107
Courtesy of M.A.P.: 26, 33, 101
Courtesy of *Men's Health*: 112
Courtesy of Microzine: 89, 90
Courtesy of Motorola: 111
Courtesy of Nike: 117
Courtesy of powerHouse Books: 96
Courtesy of Puma: 3, 87, 88, 97
Courtesy of SOPHNET.: 119, 120, 121, 122, 123, 124, 125, 126
Courtesy of Speedo® Fastskin™: 23
Courtesy of Steven Vogel: 98, 99
Courtesy of Tommy Hilfiger: 1
Courtesy of UCS: 93, 94
Courtesy of Umbro: 38
Courtesy of *Vogue Italia*: 63
Edward Steichen/Vogue, © Condé Nast Publications Inc.: 18
© Empics: 21, 22, 105
Extrait du calendrier DIEVX DV STADE 2007 – disponible sur www.stade.fr: 113, 114
© Getty Images: 14, 58, 65, 67, 70, 72, 77, 78, 103, 104, 115, 118
© JapaneseStreets.com: 75
© Nottingham Trent University: 45, 46, 47, 48, 49, 50, 51, 52
© PYMCA: 34, 64, 66, 81
© V&A Images: 6, 7, 8, 9, 10, 11, 12, 13, 15, 16, 17, 19, 20
© Yoichi Takeshi: 123, 124

FURTHER READING

Anderson, Fiona, 'Spinning the Ephemeral with the Sublime: Modernity and Landscape in Men's Fashion Textiles 1860-1900', in *Fashion Theory* (2005), vol. 9:1

Andrew, Susan, *The Design of Sports* (London, 1998)

Baker, Marc: 'Beckham: Gav's caught my gays' on icwales.co.uk (June 26, 2005), http://icwales.icnetwork. co.uk/rugbynation/rugbynews/ tm_objectid=15667479&method=full &siteid=50082&headline=beckham- gav-s-caught-my-gays-name_page.html

Barthes, Roland, *Mythologies* (London, 1993 [1957])

BBC Sport, 'New kit may be banned', http://news.bbc.co.uk/sport1/ hi/football/africa/3423231.stm (January 23, 2004)

Bedell, Geraldine, 'The changing face of the brand', in *Guardian* (January 19, 2003)

Blake, Andrew, *The Meaning of Modern Sport* (London, 1996)

Bolton, Andrew, *The Supermodern Wardrobe* (London, 2002)

Breward, Christopher, *Fashion* (Oxford, 2003)

Breward, Christopher, *Fashioning London* (Oxford, 2004)

Busch, Aikiko, *Design for Sport* (London and New York, 1998)

Campbell Warner, Patricia, *When the Girls came Out to Play: The Birth of American Sportswear* (Amherst, 2006)

Carter, Michael, *Fashion Classics: from Carlyle to Barthes* (Oxford, 2003)

Craik, Jennifer, *Uniforms Exposed: From Conformity to Transgression* (Oxford, 2005)

Cunnington, P. and Mansfield, A., *English Costume for Sports and Outdoor Recreation* (London, 1969)

Gilbert, David, 'Urban Outfitting. The city and the spaces of fashion culture', in Stella Bruzzi and Pamela Church Gibson (eds), *Fashion Cultures* (London, 2000)

Gladwell, Malcolm, 'The Coolhunt', In *The New Yorker* (March 17, 1997)

Hargreaves, John, *Sport, Power and Culture: A Social and Historical Analysis of Popular Sports in Britain* (Cambridge, 1986)

Hewitt, P. and Baxter, M., *The Fashion of Football* (London, 2006)

Holt, R. and Mason, T., *Sport in Britain 1945–2000* (Oxford, 2000)

Horne, John, *Sport in Consumer Culture* (London, 2006)

Horwood, Catherine, 'Dressing Like a Champion: Women's Tennis Wear in Interwar England', in Breward, C., Conekin, B., and Cox, C., (eds), *The Englishness of English Dress* (Oxford, 2002)

Jobling, Paul, *Man Appeal: Advertising, Modernism and Menswear* (London, 2005)

Johnston, Lucy, *Nineteenth-Century Fashion in Detail* (London, 2005)

Laver, James, *Costume and Fashion: A Concise History* (London, 1995 [1969])

Lehmann, Ulrich, *Tigersprung: Fashion in Modernity* (Boston, 2000)

Lipovetsky, Gilles, *The Empire of Fashion: Dressing Modern Democracy* (Princeton, 1994)

Lowerson, John, *Sport and the English Middle Classes 1870-1914* (Manchester, 1993)

Martin, Richard, *American Ingenuity. Sportswear 1930s–1970s* (New York, 1988)

Martin, R. and Khoda, H., *Splash! A History of Swimwear* (New York, 1990)

McQuaid, Matilda, *Extreme Textiles: Designing for High Performance* (London, 2005)

Miller, Toby, 'Sportsex', in *Human Game. Winners and Losers*, exhibition catalogue, Fondazione Pitti Discovery (Florence, 2006)

Muir, Hugh, 'Ashley Cole wins apology for sex slur' in *Guardian* (June 26, 2006)

O'Mahony, M. and Braddock, S., *Sportstech: Revolutionary Fabrics, Fashion & Design* (London, 2002)

Pavitt, Jane, *Brand New* (London, 2000)

Poirier, Diane, *Tennis Fashion* (Paris, 2003)

Quinn, Bradley, *Techno-Fashion* (Oxford, 2002)

Ricca, Barbara, *The Camera, Bikes and Bloomers* (Tempe, Arizona, 1983)

Rojek, Christopher, *Celebrity* (London, 2001)

Sassatelli, R., 'Fit Bodies. Fitness Culture and the Gym', in *Human Game. Winners and Losers*, exhibition catalogue, Fondazione Pitti Discovery (Florence, 2006)

Segal, Helen, *The Body Ascendant: Modernism and the Physical Imperative* (Baltimore, 1998)

Shannon, Brent, *The Cut of His Coat: Men, Dress and Consumer Culture in Britain 1860-1914* (Athens, Ohio, 2006)

Simmel, Georg, *On Individuality and Social Forms* (Chicago, 1971 [1957])

Skoggard, Ian, *Taiwan in the Modern World* (Armonk NY, 1996)

Smart, Barry, *The Sport Star: Modern Sport and the Cultural Economy of Sporting Celebrity* (London, 2005)

Smit, Barbara, *Pitch Invasion: Adidas, Puma and the Making of Modern Sport* (London, 2006)

Soper, Kate, 'Dress Needs: Reflections on the Clothed Body, Selfhood and Consumption', in Entwistle, J., and Wilson, E. (eds), *Body Dressing (Dress, Body, Culture)* (Oxford, 2001)

Stern, Radu, *Against Fashion: Clothing as Art* (Boston, 2004)

Thornton, Phil, *Casuals: Football, Fighting and Fashion* (Liverpool, 2003)

Tinling, Teddy, *Sixty Years in Tennis* (London, 1983)

Veblen, Thorstein, 'The economic theory of women's dress', in Leon Ardzrooni (ed.), *Essays in Our Changing Order* (New York, 1964)

Warwick, A. and Cavallero, D., *Fashioning the frame: boundaries, dress and the body* (Oxford, 1998)

Wilk, Christopher (ed.), *Modernism: Designing a New World* (London, 2006)

Wilson, Elizabeth, *Adorned in Dreams. Fashion and Modernity* (London, 1985)

Woodward, Kath, *Questioning Identity: Gender, class, ethnicity* (London, 2004)

Woodward, Sophie, 'Looking Good: Feeling Right', in Susanne Kuechler and Daniel Miller, *Clothing as Material Culture* (Oxford, 2005)

Woodward, Sophie, *Why Women Wear What they Wear* (Oxford, 2007)

BIOGRAPHIES

CHRISTOPHER BREWARD is Acting Head of Research at the Victoria and Albert Museum. He has written widely on the cultural history of fashion. Recent publications include *Fashion* (2003), *Fashioning London* (2004), *Fashion and Modernity* (2005), *Fashion's World Cities* (2006) and *Swinging Sixties* (2006).

KIM JONES is a British menswear designer who, since graduating with an MA in menswear from Central Saint Martins College of Art & Design, has developed a cult following for his refined, casual clothing. Since 2004, he has collaborated with Umbro on a clothing and shoe line called 'Umbro by Kim Jones'.

SUZANNE LEE is Senior Research Fellow in Fashion at Central Saint Martins College of Art & Design, University of The Arts, London. Her book, *Fashioning The Future: tomorrow's wardrobe* (2005) imagines a future wardrobe based on contemporary technology R&D. She has exhibited her own work internationally and has curated fashion for the British Council.

TAKEHARU SATO is Fashion Editor of *Monocle* magazine. Specializing in the Japanese Apparel Market, he has previously worked as fashion editor of *Smart* and *Smart Max* magazines in Tokyo Japan.

MARK SIMPSON is a journalist, broadcaster and writer specializing in pop culture, media and masculinity. He is credited with coining the term 'metrosexual' in 1994 and is the author of several books, including *Male Impersonators* (1994), *Sex Terror: Erotic Misadventures in Pop Culture* (2002) and *Saint Morrissey* (2004). His blog can be read at www.marksimpson.com.

SOPHIE WOODWARD is Research Associate at Nottingham Trent School of Art and Design and a Lecturer in Design and Visual Culture at University College for the Creative Arts. She is an anthropologist who has published on the issues of fashion as an everyday practice and gender, clothing and constructions of selfhood, and is the author of *Why Women Wear What they Wear* (2007).

OLIVER WINCHESTER is Assistant Curator of Contemporary Programmes where he manages the monthly Friday Late Programme. Before joining the V&A he worked at Christie's and the Barbican Art Gallery. Specializing in subcultural, queer and politically engaged visual culture, Oliver has worked on various exhibitions including *Araki. Self: Life: Death* and *Helen Chadwick: A Retrospective*.

INDEX

Page references in *italic* refer to illustrations